T O

_____

FROM

DATE

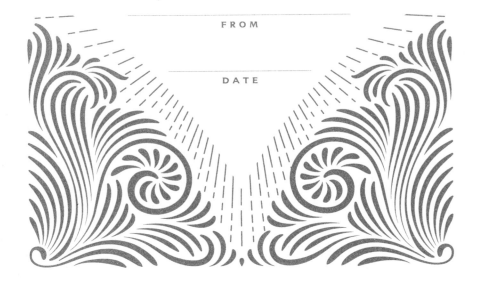

FIGHTING
WORDS

ELLIE HOLCOMB

FIGHTING WORDS

100 DAYS OF SPEAKING
TRUTH INTO THE
DARKNESS

DEVOTIONAL
EXPANDED
LIMITED EDITION

B&H
PUBLISHING
BRENTWOOD, TENNESSEE

978-1-4300-9197-4

Published by B&H Publishing Group
Brentwood, Tennessee

Dewey Decimal Classification: 242.643
Subject Heading: DEVOTIONAL LITERATURE
/ WOMEN / CHRISTIAN LIFE

Cover Design and Illustrations by Ligia Teodosiu.
Author photo by Ashtin Paige.

1 2 3 4 5 6 7 · 28 27 26 25 24

For my three children.
You are dearly loved.

ACKNOWLEDGMENTS

Annie, my fighting words friend, it has been a joy to kick back at the shadows with you all these years.

Sam, you know me, you fight for me, and you fought to make this book a reality. Thank you for your vision, tenacity, and constant support. You and your team literally make my dreams come true.

Ashley, my editor and newfound friend, you heard my heart and helped me speak it well. Thank you.

Mom, you have prayed God's Word over me and my siblings for as long as I can remember. Thank you. I treasure God's Word because I saw you treasure it first. Mom and Nancy, thank you both for living authentically head over heels for Jesus right in front of me.

My Bible study gals, thank you for delighting in God's promises with me all these years. I know Him more because I know each of you.

Drew, you breathe courage into me and help me remember what's true on the days I forget. I'm forever grateful for you.

To Maddie and our team of caretakers, thank you for loving us by loving our children so well.

To my precious friends and family, thank you for doing life with me and for all the ways each of you point me to Jesus.

To my Fighting Words Friday community, thank you for joining me on the journey of holding on to the truth for all these years and for reminding me regularly that none of us do this life alone.

A WORD FROM ELLIE ON THE EXPANDED, LIMITED EDITION

Hello to my fellow sojourners! It has been such a delight to hear from so many who have picked up the original *Fighting Words* devotional and found comfort and hope in the promises of God laid out on each page. It's been even more wonderful hearing stories from so many people who have taken me up on the invitation to memorize Scripture. Hearing how God has spoken through His Word to so many of you through this book has been a gift I'll never stop treasuring. I'm smiling wide with some of these stories running through my mind as I type this, so it is with great joy and a smile stretched across my face that I welcome you now to this special edition of *Fighting Words*.

I'm so glad you're here. This new edition carries a few treasures for you: ten extra devotionals, a lovely new cover, new interior flourishes and designs you'll only find in this edition, and one more beautifully printed Scripture memory art piece, which invites you to hide even more of God's Word in your heart.

Why ten more devotionals now? Quite frankly, I didn't realize how this book would become for me like a stack of Ebenezer stones made out of paper and ink, each Scripture passage reminding me of how God has met me, encouraged me, and transformed my forgetful heart through His Word. I also realized that there were some "lifer" verses, as one of my grandmother's calls them, that I didn't include in the first edition. "Lifer" verses are the ones that have anchored me through the storms and shadows over the years. If they were stones, they'd be smooth from years of my carrying them around in my pocket and reaching for them in moments where I desperately needed to be reminded of love and truth. There have also been other passages that have grounded songs I've written and have found their way to grounding me over the past few years. I found myself in shock that I didn't include them, so they're here now!

In my journey of memorizing Scripture, I've continued to find that God's Word is both an anchor that grounds me and a song that lifts my eyes from the valley in front of me to the One who is with me in every valley. The Scripture I've memorized and buried in my heart continues to bear fruit in my life. It keeps bringing hope, light, and comfort in the midst of days where patience runs short and especially on the days when it has felt that sorrow might swallow me whole.

As I have held onto God's promises, I find over and over again that these precious words hold onto me. My prayer for this expanded edition of *Fighting Words* is that you might find yourself upheld and uplifted by God's Word and God's Spirit in the same way I've felt upheld as I've carried these truths around in my heart. I'm so glad you're here, holding onto the light with me, and fighting the lies that so often assail us, with the strong and steady support of God's Word.

If you don't already know, and as you'll read in the "How to Use this Devotional" section of this book on page 5, I'm a singer-song-writer, which means Scripture that I love and am trying to memorize usually finds its way into a song. Singing God's Word has helped some of these truths sink deep down into my soul. You'll find that some of these additional verses in this expanded edition have grounded songs I've written like "I Will Carry You" and "I Don't Want to Miss It." Others have helped bring comfort to me during a very heavy season of loss in our community. If you'd like to sing these Scriptures along with me, I invite you to find me online where I'm often singing the truths that I need my forgetful heart to hold onto, singing the truths that end up holding onto me. I've also recorded a little Psalms project called *All of My Days* as a musical companion to this book. I've written melodies for some of the psalms I've added in this new edition, as well as a few of my other favorites to help myself sing the truth into the darkness (they are noted at the end of the devotions with a 🎵 on Days 17, 21, 59, 101, 105, 109, and 110). I love imagining that you'll listen and then join me in singing these beautiful promises of God over your own heart and the weary world around you.

I hope you'll come as you are to the wonders of God's Word with me and find comfort, light, truth, and hope on these pages. I can't wait to hear the stories Love will write in you as you meditate on and memorize and maybe even sing the promises of God alongside me. Cheers to the truth that sets us free and transforms us to be more like the One who made us and loves us perfectly.

Love,
Ellie

INTRODUCTION

There are some stories that change your life. This is one of them for me.

Thirteen years ago, I was sitting across the table from a friend of mine who battles depression. As I listened to this friend share her heart with me, I was struck by how many lies she was believing.

Lies about who she was.

Lies about who God was.

Lies about how He loved us.

And the more I listened to her talk, the more I realized that there were so many lies I was believing too . . .

All of the sudden, my heart was pounding in my chest. I started to get angry because I remembered that there is an enemy, and he's called the father of lies (John 8:44). What does that mean? It means that when he speaks, lies are his native language—that *punk*.

I remember sitting there with my friend and thinking, "I am so sick of the enemy stealing our joy, our peace, our hope, our John 10:10 'life to the full' that God came to offer us, and I am *not* going down without a fight! God calls His Word a sword, and we're gonna use it!"

In that moment, I realized that it might not be enough to just acknowledge the lies we so often believe. More than that, we desperately needed to ground ourselves in the *truth*.

I grabbed my Bible and did what sometimes you do when you feel desperate for truth: I started flipping through the pages looking for *anything* I had ever underlined before because I thought, "If I underlined it at some point, it must be good!" I remember almost shouting at my friend as I frantically flipped through my Bible, "WRITE THESE DOWN!"

It all makes me laugh now, because I was being awfully bossy, but my friend scribbled down the reference to every verse I spoke. I remember saying, "We are gonna start memorizing these verses together. These are gonna be our *fighting words*, and we're going to use 'em when the enemy comes to steal, kill, and destroy. We're gonna kick back at the darkness with the light."

So we started memorizing Scripture, and truth be told, we're not very good at it. (Insert cry-laughing face here.) But I can tell you this for sure: God's Word changed us. It didn't necessarily change our circumstances, but it changed us from the inside out because it gave us solid ground to stand on when the shame storms started rolling in. It was a shelter and a shield and an anchor and a light and a balm and a song that we began to sing into the shadows. We realized that God isn't lying when He says that His Word is alive and active, sharper than any double-edged sword. He isn't blowing smoke when He says that just like the rains that fall from the heavens don't return to the heavens until they cause the earth to bud and flourish, so is the word that goes out of His mouth. It *will* accomplish the purposes for which He sent it (Isa. 55:10–11). Y'all! That is a PROMISE, and I dare you to believe it. It will change your life. It's for sure changed mine.

I won't pretend to understand it all. God's Word is confounding and mysterious to me at times, but it also tells the most beautiful story I know: the story of a lowly God-man who entered our mess of a world so that we could know we're *never* alone and that our brokenness and suffering never have the final word. The story of a God who loves us enough to not leave us as we are, and who invites us into being a part of something much bigger than ourselves . . . a kingdom that's coming. At the end of the day, even though I don't always understand everything in the Bible, what I have experienced is this: God's Word is alive, and it's brought me to life over and over again, which is what brings us here.

I don't know how this book got into your hands. I don't know where you are on the journey. Maybe you're struggling through a season of dreams that didn't come true. Maybe you're battling depression yourself or someone you love is deeply hurting. Maybe you are weary and wounded and angry that God hasn't seemed to follow through for you. Maybe you're just busy and tired of moving aimlessly from thing to thing on your to-do list. Maybe you feel burnt out or burned by the church. Maybe you feel trapped, or maybe you just want more than what you've experienced with God and with this life that so often breaks your heart. Maybe you're a mom with young kids and you love them, but you feel like you've lost yourself as you've cared for them. Maybe you want to be a mom but can't get pregnant.

Maybe you are exhausted. Maybe you're lonely. Maybe you just want some truth to help get you through your crazy day.

Whoever you are and wherever you're coming from, I'm so glad you're here. These pages hold my fighting words. They hold the promises of God that I have clung to over the years, that have grounded me when I felt lost, and that have filled me with hope when I felt hopeless.

I hope you'll pick up these verses and hold onto them with all you've got.

I hope you'll use them to kick back at the shadows with the light.

I hope you'll let the promises on these pages sink deep into your heart.

I hope you'll have the courage to memorize a few of them with me, so that no matter where you are, you'll have the truth to cover, guide, and comfort.

I hope that these verses will become your fighting words, and that we'll all start walking right up to the darkness in our own hearts and in the weary world around us to speak God's love and light and truth.

I can't wait to see how God shows up for you, to hear how His Word leads, consoles, calms, heals, and transforms you. Maybe I'll meet you someday and get to hear stories of how you've found fighting words of your own, and how they've helped remind you that there's hope for sure, and that you have a God who loves you, cherishes you, and helps you fight the good fight.

"You will know the truth, and the truth will set you free."

JOHN 8:32

HOW TO USE
THIS DEVOTIONAL

Dear Fellow Sojourner,

This is the part of the book where I look you in the eyes. Pretend we're in my kitchen . . . this is where all my favorite conversations happen. We also have good coffee in hand. You also look great. Okay, here's my pep talk/what I want to say: I love you.

This book you're holding? It isn't really a book. It's an invitation. I'm inviting you to join me for a 100-day journey of anchoring down in the promises of God. Here's the game plan. I'm feeling like a coach today, so I've got 3 P's for you:

PROMISES

These pages hold 100 different verses and promises of God that have grounded me over the years. I've printed them out for you on every day so you can return to them again and again. We'll hold onto these truths together.

PROCESS AND PRAY

I'll process how each verse has encouraged, transformed, or comforted me, but I've included questions to invite you into the processing. In my mind, the main content of this book is God's Word—and YOUR HEART! God's Word is alive, but He also gives us a Guide, the Holy Spirit, whose role is to guide us into all truth (John 16:13). I hope you'll take time to really process these promises of God, whether that looks like prayer, journaling, pouring out your heart, or writing out the truth so you can come back to it for perspective when the lies start creeping in. I encourage you to invite the Spirit to lead you on this journey as He instills these truths down deep in your heart, like a balm to the places that need healing, like light to the places that are covered up in shadows. (Also . . . I'm not the boss of you, but I'd encourage you to have a journal at the ready so you can engage with God's Word as you're reading through and keep a record of all the good things He is showing you!)

PERMANENCE

You'll find ten pages in this book with verses beautifully printed on them. These are ten different invitations to Scripture memorization. God's Word is a treasure, and I want to invite you to bury some of it in your heart. Don't feel like you have to memorize these perfectly, but what might happen if you simply made an effort to try? I left a space next to each of these verses for you to write down the stories of how that specific promise has brought life and light to your life as you commit it to memory. It's like you'll have a permanent supply of light and hope to reach for, even through your darkest nights. (I'd also like to add here in a whisper that it has helped me so much to memorize Scripture in the context of community. Ask a friend to join you in the memorizing . . . that way you've got some accountability and someone to share the wonderful stories of how God uses this verse for flourishing in your life. I think this makes the whole process even more fun.)

I've got one last note before we dive into this adventure together. You may not know this, but I'm a musician. You'll find in this devotional that I end up quoting or referencing my own songs a lot. I hope you know that I only do that because my songs are like journals that chronicle my wrestling with God, my deepest aches, my darkest doubts, and the ways that I've tried to let the truth shine light into those weary and wounded places in my own story. So if I reference my own song, please know I'm not trying to sell you anything or say that my music is something you need in your life. I'm simply saying that I needed to write, sing, pray, or believe it for myself. Don't get me wrong, I always hope the songs I write will be sweet reminders of God's truth to all who hear them, including you; but I just need you to know I'm not trying to get you to buy my records. When I make connections to songs I've written, I'm wanting to connect you to the way God has used His Word to revive my heart again and again.

I can't wait to hear all the stories of how God shows up as you invite the Spirit to be your guide and steep your soul in God's living Word! If you could see me now, I'd be beaming . . . eyes lit up with the kind of excitement that comes when you know something good is in store.

Blessings on the journey.

Love, Ellie

DAY
1

Rejoice in the Lord always. I will say it again: Rejoice! Let
your gentleness be evident to all. The Lord is near. Don't
worry about anything, but in everything, through prayer and
petition with thanksgiving, present your requests to God.
And the peace of God, which surpasses all understanding,
will guard your hearts and minds in Christ Jesus.

PHILIPPIANS 4:4–7 CSB

I love this promise from God's Word, but the command "Rejoice in the Lord always" can sometimes feel cruel in light of some of the pain and suffering life can throw at us. There are times when I wonder, "I'm supposed to rejoice in the middle of this mess?! I don't feel like rejoicing. I feel like weeping." But then crashing into that command to rejoice is one of the sweetest promises of all: "The Lord is near."

The nearness of God has been a balm to my weary and wounded soul over and over again, and when I remember that God promises He'll be near me always, I don't have to worry, and I always have a reason to sing and to rejoice. In fact, this is the verse that inspired "Find You Here," the song I wrote in the wake of my dad's cancer diagnosis.

Nobody is ever ready for that call. A week after receiving that very scary news, my mom and dad had a worship night at their house. I'll never forget it. I stood at the edge of the room that night, almost frozen in fear, but as I watched my mom and dad run into all the darkness and all the unknown ahead of them on this cancer journey with their hands raised in the air, praising God, the invitation to join them was almost irresistible. I ended up in the middle of the room praising God right beside them, and we encountered the peace and the presence of God that night in a way that will mark me forever. We didn't have any answers or guarantees about my dad's health. But we had peace. The Lord was near. I wrote these words to "Find You Here" the next day:

It's not the news that any of us hoped that we would hear
It's not the road we would have chosen
The only thing that we can see is darkness up ahead,
But You're asking us to lay our worries
down and sing a song instead

And I didn't know I'd find You here
In the middle of my deepest fear
But You are drawing near, You are overwhelming me with peace

My dad is now cancer-free, and we're all so grateful, but I know my parents would have me say two things in light of their story: 1) Not all hard stories end this way (My family knows this well even in our own family history outside of my dad's journey.); and 2) There are no guarantees except for the faithfulness and love of Jesus, which has seen us through all the way to the cross and beyond into resurrection life that is waiting for us on the other side. Because we have that, we can look suffering dead in the eye and say, "I see you, but because of who Jesus is and because of what He did on the cross and because He walked out of the grave, you do not get the final word. Love wins in the end, and this is why we can 'rejoice always.' This is why we've always got a reason to sing."

I'm so grateful that God's promises are not only true today and every day for us, but they infuse us with the strength we need to keep rejoicing right in the face of our worries. We may be tempted to believe the lies that God isn't with us, that worrying will do more than approaching Him in prayer, that joy just isn't possible in this place. But here's the truth: *God is near*. He promises that, and in His presence, as we lay our needs and heart before Him, we can have both joy and peace. We really can. Lord, may Your nearness grant us peace and joy in the most unexpected places, even today.

- What circumstances in your life make it difficult to "rejoice always"?

- Have you ever experienced a peace or nearness from God that was unexplainable to your friends and family? What was that like?

- I've heard Beth Moore say that these verses are like God's prescription for peace. Take some time and write down the opposite of this truth. (For example, you could start off with "Complain in the Lord always. I will say it again: Complain!") After you do this, take inventory. Does your life look like you are taking a prescription for peace or for anxiety?

🔥 Father, I pray You'll grant me trust that You are near me in the midst of my worries, give me courage to present my needs and heart before You in total honesty, and infuse me with a deep gratitude that shifts my perspective in a drastic way. I thank You for the promise of peace that will come when I choose to rejoice in who You are no matter what I face.

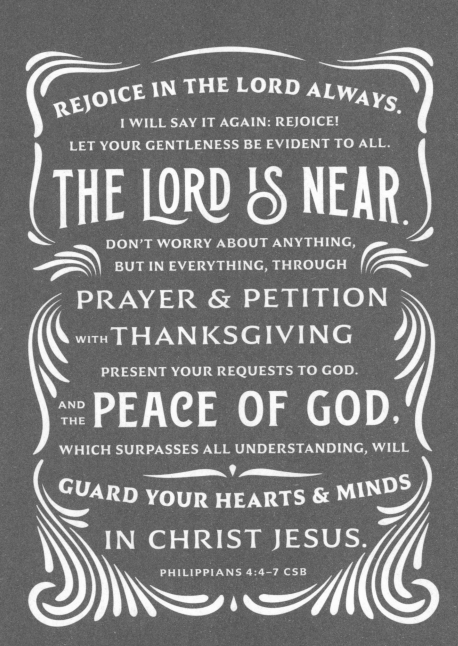

REJOICE IN THE LORD ALWAYS.
I WILL SAY IT AGAIN: REJOICE!
LET YOUR GENTLENESS BE EVIDENT TO ALL.

THE LORD IS NEAR.

DON'T WORRY ABOUT ANYTHING,
BUT IN EVERYTHING, THROUGH

PRAYER & PETITION

with THANKSGIVING

PRESENT YOUR REQUESTS TO GOD.

AND the PEACE OF GOD,

WHICH SURPASSES ALL UNDERSTANDING, WILL

GUARD YOUR HEARTS & MINDS

IN CHRIST JESUS.

PHILIPPIANS 4:4–7 CSB

DAY
2

Let the morning bring me word of your unfailing
love, for I have put my trust in you. Show me the
way I should go, for to you I entrust my life.

PSALM 143:8

So often I begin my days thinking through all the things that need
to be done and all the things I've left undone. Is this sometimes true
for you too? Don't get me wrong. I love knocking out a to-do list, but
there are many days that I end up with a pile of unchecked boxes.
Some days it feels like I'll never be able to get enough done to feel
at peace. There are loose ends that need tying up, and balls that get
dropped.

Beginning my days with the intention of all I will accomplish in a
day usually sets me up for failure. It's not that this intention is bad.
It's just that when I start my days like that, I end up measuring my
worth by how much I get done or by how many boxes I check off that
day; and if that's where my worth or value is coming from, it is far
from secure.

I love how this prayer from Psalm 143 flips all of that on its head.
Instead of beginning my days with a goal I need to reach to prove my
worth or value, I can begin my day remembering that I am a beloved
child, held in the arms of Unfailing Love. Instead of putting my hope
in my ability to handle "all the things," I can put my hope in the One
who holds all things together in the palm of His hand. What if the first
thing we meditated on in the morning was God's trustworthiness and
His powerful ability to lead us by His Spirit at every turn? What if that
was our starting place?

The good news for us is that it can be. Each morning, the sun
comes up, reminding us that God's unfailing love is waiting for us,
and that His Spirit is able to show us the way we should go. A love like

this? It won't ever fail, no matter what the to-do list looks like. What might happen if we began our days drenched in the love of God, and had open hands and hearts to simply go where He leads?

- How do you typically start your days?

- What sort of messages come flooding in your mind when you wake up in the morning?

- How can you ensure that your heart and mind hear a "word of God's unfailing love" on a daily basis?

Lord, help me to begin my days reminding my forgetful soul of Your unfailing love. And from that place of knowing I'm loved, would You lead me through each moment and remind me that my trust is not in myself or in others or in my circumstances, but in You? I surrender my moments and my time to You today.

DAY
3

"I am the light of the world. Whoever follows me will
never walk in darkness, but will have the light of life."

JOHN 8:12

This verse from John reminds me of a day I'll never forget. We were visiting our cousin, who homeschools her children in Texas, and I overheard her read this verse from Psalm 139 to her children:

"If I say, 'Surely the darkness will hide me and the light become night around me,' even the darkness will not be dark to you; the night will shine like the day, for darkness is as light to you" (Ps. 139:11–12).

She asked her boys, "If y'all are in a dark room, and you turn on a flashlight, what are you going to see?" They both piped in energetically, "The light!!" She said, "That's right, boys, don't you ever forget that the light is *always* stronger than the darkness."

That simple and beautiful truth has stuck with me over the years. It has deeply encouraged me on some of the dark nights of the soul that I've walked through. It's also been a truth I've shared with younger kids in my life. I'll never forget the day I was explaining to a few six-year-old boys that light was always stronger than the darkness, and how they did *not* believe me! So I had them go test it out. I found a flashlight and said, "Go take this and turn it on in every dark place you can think of and let me know what you see!"

So they took that flashlight inside closets, under couches, and in bathrooms with the lights turned off. And you know what? *Every* time, they would scream, "Ellie!! The light IS stronger! We can see it!!"

I wrote a song about this on one of my kids' EPs called "Light's Always Stronger." And really, I wrote it for every person, big and small, who has felt overwhelmed or lost in the darkness at times. My prayer is that the song itself—and this beautiful verse that inspired the song from John 8:12—would remind us all that there is always hope because of Jesus. Here's the chorus of that song. This is truth that I need to sing to myself over and over again, especially when I'm walking through those dark nights of the soul:

> *The light is strong*
> *Nothing can keep it from shining*
> *Even here, here in the darkest night*
> *No matter what, nothing can keep it from shining*
> *No matter how scared we are,*
> *The light's always stronger.*
> *The light's always stronger than the dark.*

He's the Light of the world who shines bright, no matter how dark the night gets. What if we really believed that about Jesus today? What if we spoke this truth into the dark places of our souls and lives, and watched just how strong the light of Christ can be for us? What if we held onto this verse, and spoke it into our loneliest nights, our deepest fears, and our hardest circumstances? I believe that we'd start exclaiming with a child-like, giddy delight,

"The light is stronger! We can see it!"

- Why do you think it's sometimes so hard to believe that light can overpower darkness?

- In what certain situations do you sometimes choose to dwell in the dark instead of walking in the light?

- How has Jesus been the "light of life" for you? How have you seen Him be "stronger" than the darkness for you?

Lord, help me follow You, so that even in my darkest nights, I will have the "light of life." Help me remember that Jesus is the Light of the world, and that He can scatter any darkness even when it feels like it's closing in around me.

Jesus answered, *"It is written*: 'Man shall
not live on bread alone, but on every word
that comes from the mouth of God.'"

MATTHEW 4:4, emphasis mine

Right after Jesus is baptized in the Jordan River, when the Spirit descends like a dove on Him and God says, "This is my Son, whom I love; with him I am well pleased" (Matt. 3:17), we read that Jesus is then led by the Spirit into the wilderness to be tempted by the devil (Matt. 4:1). I'm not sure about you, but this does not sound like the way we have celebrated baptisms in my family! It's been forty days of fasting, and the enemy comes in with lies and temptations . . . isn't that just like Satan? Coming in for the attack when we are tired, weary, lonely, and even hungry. (If it were me, I would have been HANGRY . . . the angry kind of hungry, if you know what I mean.)

This passage has always been hard for me to wrap my head around. Why on earth would Jesus begin His active ministry on earth after His baptism by wandering alone in the desert, being tempted by Satan? When I started memorizing Scripture over a decade ago, I remember telling my friend Sara how powerful it had been for me to be able to fight so many of the lies that I believe with God's Word. I'll never forget how she responded. She said, "That makes total sense. That's how Jesus fought the lies of the enemy too. Remember in the desert? He's out there for forty days wandering, hungry, and to every lie that the enemy whispers, Jesus responds with 'It is written . . .' and then He quotes Scripture. So really, you're just following in His footsteps!"

My mouth dropped open. Of course Jesus would do this for us. He went first. He wandered in the wilderness and modeled what it looks like to shut down the attempts of the enemy for us. The weapon of choice? God's Word. "It is written." If Jesus used the Word of God to silence the enemy's lies, then that must mean that we can and should use God's Word in the same way, for we do "not live on bread alone, but on every word that comes from the mouth of God" (Matt. 4:4).

Let's continue to feed our souls the words that come from the mouth of God, and hold tight to them when the enemy comes with every kind of lie or temptation. Thank You, God, that You provide for us, both physically and spiritually. Help us feast on Your Word and follow in the footsteps of Jesus, speaking the truth even when we're lost in the wilderness.

- Describe a time in your life that felt like wandering in the wilderness. Were there any lies about God or yourself that you were tempted to believe, especially as you were walking through a seemingly desolate place?

- Make a list of some of the lies you are prone to believe about yourself and about God, especially during wilderness seasons (if you can do this on notecards, even better!).

- For every lie you write down, go find a verse that speaks truth over that lie. If you wrote the lies on notecards, write the truth on the back of the card. I call this an "It is Written" list, and it has been such a beautiful way for me to speak light into the darkness of the lies I am so prone to believe. These are generally good verses to memorize as well, so you have them tucked in your heart for easy access when you need them the most.

🔥 Thank You, God, that when we walk through wilderness seasons, we are not alone. Thank You for Your Word that speaks a stronger truth over any lie we'll ever be tempted to believe, and thank You for Your Son, the LIVING Word, who modeled out for us the way to hold onto the truth and speak it into the darkness. Help me to fight the lies that I so often believe with the truth from Your Word.

DAY
5

"I have it all planned out.
Plans to take care of you, not abandon you.
Plans to give you the future you hope for."

JEREMIAH 29:11 MSG

Remember that famous scene in *The Lion, the Witch, and the Wardrobe* from The Chronicles of Narnia series? The one where Susan is surprised that the king of Narnia is a lion, and so she asks Mr. Beaver if Aslan is a *safe* lion? The answer is one of the best lines in all of literature: "Safe? . . . Who said anything about safe? 'Course he isn't safe. But he's *good*. He's the King, I tell you."[1]

Some days I really need that reminder. Because life doesn't feel safe in every single moment. In fact, it can feel so unsafe and unsteady some days that I start wondering if God is really and truly and deeply and fully good. And, by extension, I start wondering if His *plans* are good. I'm like Susan, wondering what sort of King this really is. Is He for me? Will He abandon me? Are His plans to be trusted?

Man, if I can remember that our King is good. That God's heart toward me is kindness. That, just like this verse promises, *all* His plans for me are in my best interest. That, ultimately, His plans are good because *He* is good. Trusting these things would change the way I face my future . . . all the unknowns, and especially the way I walk through storms and trials in my life that feel shaky or unsafe.

I'm so thankful the King loves us enough to give us a hopeful future, and that His plans for us are good. When the lie closes in that tries to convince us of the opposite—that He really isn't kind or that His plans are for our harm—let's walk forward together holding on to this truth. Good kings make good plans. And our King? He's really and

19

truly and deeply and fully good. That means any plan He makes can be trusted, including the one He has for us.

- What unsteady circumstances sometimes tempt you to believe God isn't good?

- Do you believe God's heart toward you is kindness? Why or why not?

- Look back over key moments in your own story. What parts of the journey seemed like God must've had the plans all wrong—only to find out later that His plan was actually far better for you than you ever could have seen in the moment?

Lord, help me believe that You are good all the way through, and that because of this, all Your plans for me will certainly be used somehow for my good. Help me to trust Your heart for me, even when I can't see all the ways this leg of the journey will play out.

DAY 6

But now, this is what the LORD says—he who created you,
O Jacob, he who formed you, O Israel: "Fear not, for I have
redeemed you, I've called you by name, you are mine."

ISAIAH 43:1

I started memorizing the last part of this verse with my little girl when she was just two years old! She was having a hard time memorizing it, so I made up a little song and started to sing it to her. We would sing it together on the nights that the dark felt scary and she couldn't go to sleep. Sometimes it was a bad dream she had, and sometimes she was just afraid that there might be monsters under her bed.

As I've thought about my little girl's fear, I've realized that her struggle isn't isolated to childhood. Adults can live just as scared as little ones do. Instead of lurking under our bed, grown-up monsters tend to lurk in the shadows of our mind in the form of worst-case scenarios, don't they? I know that's true for me. My mom has also struggled with this. Once, when she was battling through a lot of fear, her counselor and pastor asked her this: "Debbie, what is the worst thing that could happen in this situation?"

She explained in detail what that would be, and then he said this: "Okay, if that happens—that worst-case scenario that you just laid out—would God still love you?"

She replied, "Yes."

And then he asked, "Would you still love God?"

She answered again, "Yes."

"Then I can tell you for certain that you are going to be okay because if you have the love of God to surround and support you, you can face anything."

This particular promise from God's Word helps me so much in the wildness of real life because, like that kind pastor pointed out to my mom, it doesn't guarantee that we won't be afraid or that scary circumstances will never come our way. It speaks a stronger truth into any fear that we might face. It reminds us that, even in the dark places where fear consumes us, nothing changes the fact that God has redeemed us, that He knows us, and that no matter how the story ends, we belong to Him. We are safe in Him now and forever, for His love surrounds us and supports us. Even in the worst of scenarios. *Especially* there. Singing this promise over my daughter and with her over the years has helped me lean into His safety in moments when fear is gripping me tight.

I'm so grateful that no matter how scared we are, God's love and strength will hold us tighter than fear can. If I can remember that I am held in my scariest places, it changes everything and it helps me carry on with more courage than I could ever muster up on my own

- What are some unhealthy reactions you've previously had to fear? What are some healthy reactions you've seen in yourself?

- How does it feel to know that in the middle of such scariness, God calls you by name? How does it change things to know you are His?

- Even if your worst fear came true, would it change what is true about God?

🔥 Father, thank You for meeting me in the darkness, calling me by name, and reminding me that I belong to You, even when life feels scary. Give me the strength to trust Your love in the dark, in the fear, and in the flood.

DAY
7

... And I pray that you, being rooted and established in love,
may have power, together with all the Lord's holy people,
to grasp how wide and long and high and deep is the love of
Christ, and to know this love that surpasses knowledge—that
you may be filled to the measure of all the fullness of God.

EPHESIANS 3:17–19

"Filled to the measure." That is what I want for my broken heart:
to be filled to the measure of all the fullness of God's love. Can you
imagine what the world could look like if this was true for all of us?

I have always adored this verse. I've prayed this prayer over so
many people in my life, including myself. I've seen God answer this
prayer too, time and time again, helping me and others understand
just how deep His love runs for us. Deeper than our biggest fears,
our worst failures, and our most painful wounds. Further above the
highest level of love we've ever felt for someone else. Wider than the
lengths we'd go for our own flesh and blood.

Like so many of my "fighting words" verses, it was such a joy when
I wrote this verse into a song called "Wide, High, Long, Deep" for one
of my children's EPs. Why? It's the truth that changes me the most, so
in a sense, this truth is the kind of "song" that I actually want to get
stuck in my head and my kids' heads, one that sings God's promise
of abundant love over us! So often I feel like I'm unworthy and unable
to make the mark. Unlovable and unlovely. And living in that state of
mind forces me to go out into the world, looking for something to fill
me up with value and worth and "okayness." Wherever I go for that
stuff, I find that it leaks out of my heart faster than I can put it in!
But when I go back to the foundational truth of how high and wide
and long and deep the love of God is for me—all without me trying
to make myself lovely before Him—I approach life from a place of

fullness rather emptiness, of "loved" instead of "unloved," of "valued" instead of "worthless." It fills me up to the measure, and instead of looking to the world to fill me up or validate me, I am able to walk into the world with something to give away.

This is the verse I pray over myself when I am nervous about going to a gathering or an event. Do you ever feel that way, like sometimes you walk into a scenario as an adult that makes you feel like you're smack-dab, back in a middle school cafeteria again . . . unsure of who you are, if you belong, and who to talk to or connect with? Maybe that's just me, but this verse shifts my perspective beautifully whenever I am feeling insecure. It reminds me that because of who God is, I can feel lonely, and yet I'm never really alone. I can feel awkward, and yet know that I'm embraced. I can feel unsteady about who I am and remember that even on the days I forget who I am and who God made me to be, I am grounded and anchored in Love. It's my favorite party trick, because all of the sudden my focus goes off of my insecurities to the secure and steady nature of God's love for me, and once I land there. I'm able to stop thinking about myself so much and get to the business of really seeing other people more clearly and loving them abundantly, in the same way God loves me.

Let's pray today that we would remain "rooted and established" in God's *love*. Let's think on how high and wide and deep this *love* really goes. May *love* fill in all the gaps, and as we meditate on and ground ourselves in how much He loves us, may it transform our broken hearts into cups that run over with love.

- In what areas of life do you feel unlovable or unlovely?
- In what ways do you sometimes go out into the world in search of its love and validation?
- Have you ever had a season where God's love was taking up so much space in your heart and mind that you felt "filled to the measure"? What was that like?
- How can you seek to be filled up by God's love today?

🔥 Lord, pour out Your love on me today, and help it overflow in my own heart and into the lives of others. Help me approach life from a place of Your fullness and validation instead of looking to other places to make me feel worthy. Help me grasp how wide and high and long and deep Your love is for me, because when I truly understand that, everything changes.

The Lord is my light and my salvation—whom
shall I fear? The Lord is the stronghold of
my life—of whom shall I be afraid?

PSALM 27:1

Of all my "fighting words" verses, I'll never forget how this one ended up in my life. I began memorizing this verse many years ago after someone had broken into our home and stolen our TV and some other things. Has that ever happened to you—a break-in? If so, you probably remember that day as one where it wasn't just a person who broke into your home, but when fear broke into your heart, which is something that lingers a lot longer than thieves do.

After the break-in, I was frozen in fear as I went to bed each night, but I had a friend tell me that if I would continue proclaiming God's Word, even when I didn't feel like or trust that it was true, that His Word would prevail. I said this verse out loud many nights, for months, over and over again, and still felt terrified. I wrote this verse and several others on cards and taped them up all over the house so I could be reminded of the truth, and while those cards were wonderful reminders, I still felt fearful. But one night, something finally clicked, and I felt this weight lift off of my chest because I actually started believing that God was my stronghold. If the Lord is truly the One holding onto me, then there is nothing I have to fear.

Whatever it is that is breaking into your life right now, trying to steal your joy and peace, my prayer is that you'll hold on to His promises, friend. Because when *those* break into your life, nothing can hold you captive any longer. He is faithful. He's a stronghold. He's a light. We don't have to be afraid.

- What situation in your life feels like it is "breaking in" to steal your joy and peace?

- Do you give God the same room in your life to "break in" compared to the room you allow for fear to break in? Why or why not?

- A stronghold is "a place that has been fortified so as to protect it against attack." Think of the picture of God as a stronghold. How does the image of God as a stronghold relate to the lies that try to break into your heart?

- Take some time to write this verse and a few others out on cards to hang up around your home. What might happen for you if you had reminders of the truth in front of your eyes on a regular basis?

Lord, break in. Break into my fear and my worries. Break into the places I feel paralyzed, and replace my terror with trust. Help me remember that You are my faithful stronghold, my light, no matter how deep the darkness is around me.

DAY
9

Have you ever had seasons full of pain and loss? My husband, Drew, and I walked through a season of about four years of seemingly senseless suffering and sorrow. We have a vibrant community, but in that period of time, so many different people we love dearly walked through deeply painful circumstances. We had dear friends experience everything from anxiety to depression to years of infertility to addiction to a cancer diagnosis to a divorce, and we walked with two different families who lost children. We were raw and weary as we journeyed through blow after heart-breaking blow with our people.

It was during that excruciatingly painful season that I began to cling tightly to this verse. It was such a comfort to know that even as our hearts were breaking, God broke too. He sent His Son to be broken for us so we could know we would never be alone in the brokenness. During that difficult season, we encountered the companionship and comfort of the Man of Sorrows Himself. We often didn't know the right words to pray during that season, but we did experience healing, as God met our aching hearts with His very presence, and it was this that inspired Drew and I to write the song "Man of Sorrows":

Lord, You're aching with me
Help me to believe
That when my soul is lost in the storm
You're acquainted with my grief

Man of Sorrows, what a name
Bore our suffering, bore all of our shame
Man of Sorrows, broken sinners to reclaim
You overcame the darkness, and walked out of the grave

One of our friends who lost his little boy just days after he was born has said this: "I think God's answer to suffering might be, 'Me too.'" Isn't that powerful? God suffered too. He suffered for us, so we could know that suffering never gets the final word. Jesus was broken for us, so we could know our brokenness is never the end of the story. He walked out of a grave with scars on His resurrected body, so we could know that this scarred God-man defeated death. "By his wounds, we are healed."

Lord, help us remember that this verse carries both the promise of ultimate healing, but also the promise of the companionship and comfort in the middle of our deepest places of sorrow.

- Whatever pain or loss you're facing (or have faced), how does it encourage you to know that your God deeply understands what suffering is like?

- Who are your people, and what kind of sorrows do they carry today? How might God be leading you to simply show up for them right now?

- We all face seasons of "blow after heart-breaking blow." What ultimate blow did Christ take for you? How does this truth change the way you face hard seasons?

Jesus, I praise You for choosing the way of suffering that I might have a companion in my own journey through it. You know the sorrows I carry today, and I entrust them to You right now, for You understand the depth of them even more than I do. Help me remember that You endured the greatest version of pain and loss on the cross—on my behalf! Let Your endurance through sorrow empower mine today and use me as an instrument of comfort in the lives of others.

"And surely I am with you always,
to the very end of the age."

MATTHEW 28:20

I don't know what the Covid-19 pandemic was like for you. But goodness, for me, I felt so isolated. I missed hugging people. I missed proximity to others. I missed going to concerts, being in a room full of other people singing along to songs they know and love. I missed being at church and standing in line as we waited to take communion together. I missed busy restaurants and children playing happily with other kids at the playground. I missed gathering with our friends and families on holidays and birthdays.

Maybe you missed the same things. And maybe, even today, there are a whole host of other reasons outside of a global pandemic that you feel alone. After all, viruses aren't the only things in this world that make a person feel isolated. No matter the reason behind our feelings of loneliness, Jesus speaks this truth over us loud and clear: YOU ARE NOT ALONE. I AM WITH YOU ALWAYS.

It's true. We're not alone! I know it *felt* that way for such a long time, and probably still feels that way. Pandemic or not, these days can feel isolated for so many reasons, and if you are feeling that way right now, I hope you'll lean in close to hear the truth . . . *Love is with you.*

God is love, and while you may not be able to feel Him some days, it doesn't change the truth that He's got you right in the palm of His hand. When we pray for our friends and family, a lot of times my kids will ask if we can just sing "He's got the whole world in His hands," but they put our friends' and family's names in the song. "He's got Bebe and Pop Pop in His hands." Maybe it's just the singer in me, and maybe you'll think it's silly, but I cannot *help* imagining what it would be like if we sung this over ourselves right now. Even if it seems strange at first, try singing it over yourself . . . or speaking it, if singing feels too uncomfortable for you! (Or whisper-sing if you are in a public place and do not want anyone to hear you!) No matter what, just sit in this truth for a moment:

"He's got (put your name here) in His hands!
He's got (put your name in here) in His hands!
He's got (put your name in here) in His hands!
He's got the whole world in His hands!"

I know you may not have liked how that sounded or that you might have felt too self-conscious to sing that out loud, but more than anything, I hope we can let this simple song carry a simple truth deep into our souls. I hope you can sense today that beneath you and around you are Everlasting arms, and I hope you'll lean into them and let out the sadness and fear and worry. He can take and hold it all. It's okay for us to lament and grieve what we have lost. Considering everything we have faced as a globe, it's appropriate for goodness sake; but it's also so appropriate and important to hold onto the hope that: we aren't on our own, God's got full control of the world and its future, and suffering has an expiration date!

- When Covid-19 descended upon the world, what was it like for you?

- How does Jesus' promise in this verse give you hope for today and tomorrow?

- How might you walk differently through seasons of isolation if you believed that this verse was true?

God, I feel so alone sometimes. But I give You praise and thanks for being with me always, regardless of how I feel. Thank You for holding me in Your everlasting arms, not just today, but "to the very end of the age."

If any of you lacks wisdom, you should ask
God, who gives generously to all without
finding fault, and it will be given to you.

JAMES 1:5

I cannot tell you the amount of times I've fixated on a problem, let a conflict or decision circle around and around in my head, and asked everyone and their mother what they thought that I should do about it, all in an effort to search for wisdom from the people I trust. Maybe you can relate.

I'm not saying that seeking wise counsel from others is wrong, because the wisdom of others can be a wonderful gift. But when I recently read this promise from God's Word, I was undone. So often, God seems to be the *last* person I turn to when I am really needing wisdom, and here is this promise, plain as day, saying that He gives wisdom generously to all without finding fault! He doesn't get frustrated when we don't have the wisdom we need for all the things life throws at us! This verse actually presumes that we will lack wisdom at times, and the good news is that when we ask Him for wisdom, His Word says He will give it . . . *generously.*

This verse has helped me immensely. It's not that I never ask trusted mentors and friends for advice or for wisdom anymore; it's just that God is becoming my first ask. And you know what? I've found that even the act of bringing the decision or conflict or situation before Him calms my fretful heart.

Do you need wisdom today? So do I. Let's ask God for it. He'll give it to us!

- When you evaluate your life right now, in what areas or circumstances do you lack wisdom?

- How does it feel to know that God is not frustrated with you for lacking the wisdom, but instead, desires to give it to you generously?

- In which situations of life are you seeking the wisdom of people before the wisdom of God? Why?

- How might your life and conflicts look different if God was your first ask?

🔥 God, help me remember that when I lack wisdom, You long to generously fill that lack. Give me the courage to come to You and ask you for wisdom first before seeking out the thoughts of others. In all the situations that are on my mind, please fill me with Your wisdom and send Your Word to be a "lamp for my feet, a light for my path" (Ps. 119:105).

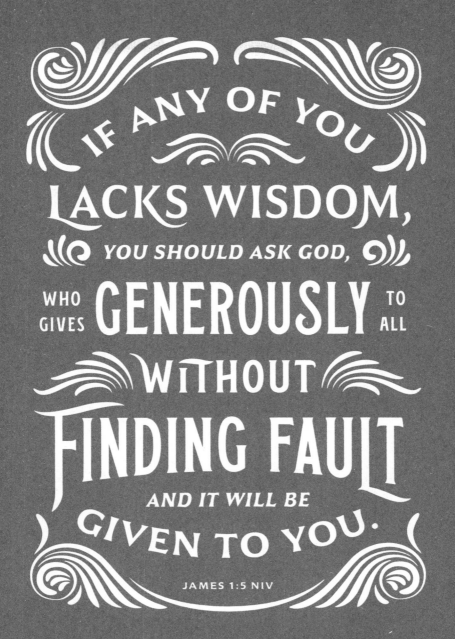

IF ANY OF YOU LACKS WISDOM, YOU SHOULD ASK GOD, WHO GIVES GENEROUSLY TO ALL WITHOUT FINDING FAULT AND IT WILL BE GIVEN TO YOU.

JAMES 1:5 NIV

DAY
12

Your kingdom is an everlasting kingdom, and your dominion endures through all generations. The LORD is trustworthy in all he promises and faithful in all he does. The LORD upholds all who fall and lifts up all who are bowed down. The eyes of all look to you, and you give them their food at the proper time. You open your hand and satisfy the desires of every living thing. The LORD is righteous in all his ways and faithful in all he does. The LORD is near to all who call on him, to all who call on him in truth. He fulfills the desires of those who fear him; he hears their cry and saves them.

PSALM 145:13–19

I don't know about you, but some days I need the reminder that, like a parent who clutches a stumbling child by the arm to prevent them from wiping out, God knows how to uphold me in the moments I fall. He's not far away. He promises to be right there beside me. He is "trustworthy" in His promises and He is "faithful" in whatever He does. He "upholds" those who fall and He "lifts up" those who are doubled over. What care and love.

And did you see all the "alls" in this passage? If you missed them, you might even take time to go back and underline each one. They have helped and encouraged my heart today. God's kingdom endures through not just one or two generations, but *all* generations. He's trustworthy in not just some of what He promises, but *all* He promises. He is faithful in not only the things we can visibly understand or see, but in *all* He does. He upholds not some of us, but *all* who fall and *all* who are bowed down. He's near to not a special few, but *all* who call on Him. What a sweet reminder, and what good news this is, for I am certainly one of the "alls" crying out for His steadying hand.

If you feel like you need to be lifted up by someone stronger than yourself, know that He's got you. Fully and completely and in *all* the ways. Thank You, Lord, for Your trustworthiness today, and help us lean into Your all-encompassing love for us.

— Which promise in this passage is ministering most to your heart today? Why?

— In what ways do you feel like you're "bowed down" these days? How do you usually handle this experience? (Do you try to get back up in your own power and striving? Do you stay on the ground, afraid that you don't deserve the chance to get back up again?)

— Reflecting on your life, how have you seen God uphold you in a moment you were stumbling? How does that past grace give you strength for today's struggle?

🔥 Father, thank You for being so trustworthy and faithful to me. Thank You for lifting me up even when I am bowed down, and for being near me in all the moments I need You. Help me to call out to You when I fall, and infuse me with trust that You always hear me, You've always got me, and You'll always answer my cries for help.

"And I tell you that you are Peter, and on this rock I will build my church, and the gates of Hades will not overcome it."

MATTHEW 16:18

Who is your favorite character in Scripture? It's so hard for me to choose. I don't know if I could name a "number one" favorite, but I do know that Peter is somewhere on the list for sure. Why? Because he's such a prime example of the promise we held onto yesterday—that God is able to uphold us, even when we're about to wipe out! Peter is constantly fumbling around in his spiritual journey, putting his foot in his mouth, and misunderstanding things, yet God still lets him experience miraculous things.

I so relate to the not-so-great moments in Peter's life. Remember how he boldly joined Jesus to walk out on the water, but took his eyes off Jesus to look at the waves around him, freaked out, and started to sink? I totally relate to this! I'm all like, "Send me, Lord!" and then as soon as it gets scary or hard, I'm praying "Just kidding, God!! Send me back . . . never mind! Not sure what on earth I was thinking. I am not the girl for the job!" Or I think about that time Peter tried to defend Jesus and, in his misguided fervor to save the day, he pulled out a sword and cut someone's ear off? (Thankfully, I've never done this, but I do sometimes feel like I take more responsibility than I need to in "defending" Jesus or trying to manage other people's thoughts about God instead of following the Lord's lead and trusting the Spirit to do the life-altering work in others' hearts. Oh Lord, forgive me for how I try to step into that role sometimes! I am NOT the Holy Spirit, as it turns out.) And of course, there's that time Peter got scared and denied Jesus after swearing that he would never deny Him. In the face of trouble, Peter got it wrong a lot of times. And I'm sure the same could be said for you and me.

But you know what encourages me most? For all of Peter's blunders, Jesus kept walking with him. He kept giving Peter new and miraculous experiences to help him grow. For example, when Peter did start sinking after walking on water, Jesus was there to take him by the hand. Peter got to see prison doors break open, and an angel of God set him free. And he was also the one who said that triumphant statement, "You are the Messiah, the Son of the living God"—the very statement Jesus turned around and responded with: "Blessed are you, Simon son of Jonah, for this was not revealed to you by flesh and blood, but by my Father in heaven. And I tell you that you are Peter, and on this rock I will build my church, and the gates of Hades will not overcome it" (Matt. 16:16–18). When we trace Peter's life, we see that as the years go by, the Lord slowly changed him from a stumbling, fumbling struggler into a wise apostle who wrote two letters in the New Testament—letters that deeply encouraged other strugglers!

Today I stand in awe that God can meet, change, and use any old stumbling soul like me. If you're in a season of not-so-great moments with the Lord, or wondering if God's promise to uphold you can really be trusted, remember the stumbling disciple we find in Peter. Remember that God still has miraculous things waiting for you, and Jesus will keep walking with you.

- Of all the characters in Scripture, who stands out to you most? Why?

- How does Peter's journey encourage you today? Where do you feel like you're fumbling and stumbling?

- Can you think of a time you made a mistake and saw Jesus meet you with grace and change you in the process?

Lord, thank You for continuing to walk with me, even when I fumble or misunderstand. Help me remember that You love to meet, change, and use me even in the midst of my stumbling.

DAY
14

"You will know the truth, and the truth will set you free."

JOHN 8:32

Have you ever watched one of those movies where, on some fateful night, a huge misunderstanding happens and the main character is wrongly accused and then, to make matters worse, wrongly imprisoned? As the story always seems to go, only the truth about "what happened that night" can set the prisoner free. Through some unexpected plot twists, the pieces of what happened come together, and it becomes clear that the prisoner shouldn't be locked in chains anymore. The truth has finally come to light, and because of that, the barred doors open. The accusations stop. The wrongly accused is allowed to go free. It's amazing to see that this is the power of the truth—*it sets people free.*

In a lot of ways, I've found that this is how the truth of God's Word works. We're the prisoner—taking the blows of accusation after accusation from the enemy, trapped in what feels like a prison of lies. He tries to keep us in chains, but because Jesus has paid for every mess and mistake, the truth is that *we don't have to keep those chains on.* Jesus has already paid for anything and everything the enemy might accuse us of. There's no debt left to be paid, no finger left to be pointed in our face. We are wrongly accused—not because we didn't mess up at some point, but because the mess is already cleaned up!

So when the enemy comes accusing, chains in hand, I pray we'll remember the truth for ourselves, and then, together, remind him of this: "all the things you are pointing at have already been charged to the account of Jesus, and He paid it all. There's nothing left here for you to point out. 'What happened that night' has been redeemed—the cross is what happened that night! Jesus is what happened! And He already paid for all of the things you're trying to heap on my head.

The matter is done and dealt with and *you have no case here.*" And just like that, the prison doors will open.

This is not to say that we don't take responsibility for our actions and mistakes, but in the same breath, we do not have to be defined by the mistakes we make because of what Jesus did for us on the cross. The accusations can't hold us down anymore. The chains drop to the ground! And we can move forward without looking back. Because that's what fighting lies with the truth of God's Word does for us—it sets us free. I'm so thankful this is true. I'm so grateful for the way the truth of God's Word and His love for us have transformed my weary and forgetful heart over and over again, especially when I'm battered by lies and accusations. Thankful for all the ways truth continues to bring freedom in my life, and your life too.

- What kinds of accusations and lies are battering you right now? What has fighting them looked like for you?

- When you feel trapped or scared, what do you usually run toward to "set you free"?

- What if you ran to Jesus when you feel accused or trapped or shamed? How might your life change if this was your first response when the enemy comes accusing?

🔥 Jesus, thank You for paying for anything and everything I might ever be accused of. Thank You for Your Word, that reminds me of this truth, and help me remember it once again when I feel trapped in chains. Give me the strength to run to You when the lies or accusations close in and give me the heart to believe that I am truly set free by Your work and Your Word.

DAY
15

Praise be to the God and Father of our Lord Jesus Christ,
the Father of compassion and the God of all comfort.

2 CORINTHIANS 1:3

This world can feel so heavy some days. Whether it's the news channel telling countless tragic stories, or our own lives that are so often full of struggle, conflict, loss, doubt, loneliness, and desire unfulfilled, life can feel overwhelming.

I love that speaking right in the face of all of the pain and struggle and heartache that we so often experience is this declaration of truth: the One who made us is the Father of compassion and the God of all comfort. That means there is no such thing as a tragedy He can't console. There's no such thing as a struggle He can't strengthen us in. There's no such thing as a conflict He can't help us resolve. There's no such thing as a loss He can't comfort us through. There's no such thing as a wound He cannot heal.

Having the "God of all comfort" as our Lord means that no matter how far down the road of doubt we've traveled, He can meet us there. No matter how gaping the hole of our longing, He can fill it. No matter how deep the pain, He can reach it. That's the wonder of our God. This is the verse I grounded my song "God of All Comfort" in, and it's a song I often listen to on the days I'm overwhelmed by the weight of the world.

No one's too far. No one's too broken.
God says His heart is full of compassion
Everlasting arms hold us together
When we're falling apart
He is the God of all comfort

Lord, help us remember today that when our hearts are weighed down, we can run fast toward Your comfort, enjoying Your tender care and consolation.

- Instead of trying to be strong on your own, what's something you might need to let God comfort you in right now?

- We know God is our Father in general, but what insights come to mind as you think about God particularly as the "Father of *compassion*"?

- If today does not feel heavy to you, who in your life might be bearing a heavy load? Use the space below to pray this verse over them today.

Father, thank You for being a God of compassion and comfort. Help me remember that You desire to console me in the hard places, and give me the strength to surrender those hard places to Your kind comfort even now.

DAY
16

Sing to GOD a brand-new song.
He's made a world of wonders!

PSALM 98:1 MSG

Can you remember a childhood gift that really captured your awe and wonder—leaving you open-mouthed with stars in your eyes? Not too long ago, one of these kinds of gifts captivated our whole family. I bought my son a cup of caterpillars for his birthday. We fed them, watched them grow to seven times their size, marveled as they spun their cocoons, and waited with great anticipation for the incredible transformation to happen. It felt like watching a miracle unfold in our very own kitchen. And that's just *one* of God's mysterious and amazing works we get to discover and stand in awe over as we look around at His creation.

I'm so grateful for this "world of wonders" that we live in, and that in so many ways, creation whispers the truth to us about God's redemption and beauty. It's like God wrote a love letter into the fabric of the earth to ever-remind us of who He is and how He loves us: the caterpillar takes flight and helps us remember that God has the power to transform us, the stars whisper about the Light of the World, Himself, who is with us even in our darkest nights. Trees that look dead in the winter begin to hum and burst into spring-green life, reminding us that because of God's amazing gospel work in Christ, death always gives way to life. What beautiful imagery this "world of wonders" gives to us, reminding us daily that we *always* have a reason to lift up a brand-new song to our God.

I love this concept so much that I wrote a children's book about it called *Who Sang the First Song?* and a whole record of songs inspired by God's creation that all point back to Him and invite listeners and readers, young and old, to sing along with the marvelous song the earth is singing about our Maker each day.

Here's hoping that today and every day we won't miss out on tuning into creation's beautiful song, and turning around to sing it back to our Creator.

- When was the last time you found yourself totally captivated by something in creation?

- If you can't remember the last time this happened, what do you think distracts you from noticing the "world of wonders" God has made?

- What usually helps you focus on the song creation sings about the Lord? What would it look like to "turn the volume up" on the song creation sings each day to help you see and hear it better?

🔥 God, thank You for making a "world of wonders" that sings about You! Open my eyes and ears to hear it today and remove any distractions that would keep me from listening well and singing a brand-new song of wonder-struck gratitude back to You, the One who made me and the beautiful world around me.

Israel, put your hope in the LORD, for with the LORD
is unfailing love and with him is full redemption.

PSALM 130:7

Where do you tend to place your hope? I don't know about you, but SO many days I put my hope in my own capability to carry my own burdens, and the burdens of other people that I love. I'll just pile it all on my shoulders, trying to control it, trying to make everything work out in the way I think is best. I might even pray for God to intervene, but only in the ways I think He should.

As it turns out, these are not the kinds of prayers that help me place my hope in the Lord. So many days I step into life as if I am the rescuer or the one who can make things right instead of carrying my burdens and the burdens of others to the foot of the cross. Eventually, I burn out. I stumble. I fall, and so often it's from this humbling place that I remember to put my hope in the Lord.

Why on earth would I trust my own fumbling hands over His? With Him is love abounding and full redemption.

This is one of the verses that inspired my song "Only Hope I've Got:"

I don't want to tell some arrogant story
or let myself believe I'm You
I don't want to be a thief who's stealing Your glory
So help remind me of what is true, that
the only Hope I've got is You

I don't want to try to do what God can only do. I don't want to place my hope in my own strength. I want to place my hope in the One who offers "full redemption" . . . what a promise. I don't understand how that works itself out all the time. I know we are redeemed by God right this very minute in His sight, but I also know that we still live in a very broken world. On the days I get overwhelmed by the burdens I carry and by the pain and suffering in this world, I call to mind that one day, a *full redemption* of the whole world is coming. One day, "all the sad things are going to come untrue," as Tolkien would say.[2] May we lay our burdens down, and put our hope in the One who will one day renew *all* things. Lord, help us to remember on the days we forget that it's true, that the only hope we've got is *You*.

- Where do you tend to place your hope?
- What burdens are you hoping you'll be able to manage in your own strength right now?
- What would it look like to lay those burdens down and place your hope in God's unfailing love and capability to bring full redemption today?

🔥 Lord, I cry out to You right now with the burdens and needs I carry. Thank You for making a way, through the cross, for me to access Your love and grace any time I need it! Help me to place my hope in Your unfailing love.

If you'd like to sing this psalm with me, it's written into the song called "Wait for You" on my album, *All of My Days*.

DAY
18

Give ear to my words, O LORD, consider my sighing. Listen
to my cry for help, my King and my God, for to you I pray.
In the morning, O LORD, you hear my voice; in the morning
I lay my requests before you and wait in expectation.

PSALM 5:1–3

Maybe you've been in some sort of setting—in church, at an event, in a Bible study, perhaps—where you heard someone pray, and you just loved it. It was real. It was raw. It felt like a real-life *human* engaging with a trusted friend instead of a religious robot spouting off spiritual one-liners. Maybe you thought, "Wow—this makes me want to *pray*."

These words from David in Psalm 5 are like that for me. I *love* his earnest prayer. I think I'm drawn to his words because there are so many days that I, too, feel like I am crying out for help from the Lord. There are also days when I choose to try to muster up my own strength and go it alone, but it is always better when I pray.

What encourages me most about prayer is that it so often shifts my perspective from the problem in front of me to the One who holds the world in His hands, from the mountain I am facing, to the One who can move mountains. "O LORD." "My King." "My God." And again, "O LORD." Four different times in just three verses, David directs his heart's cry not to himself or anyone else, but to *the Lord*. How different would my life be if I always directed my cries to God? Another reason I love this prayer is that it helps me "wait in expectation" to see how the Lord I am crying out to will intersect with every place of pain, fear, worry, and struggle in my life. Expectation means we believe our God *does something* with our requests! We can't be certain *what* He will do with them, but we know that because He's the living God and because He's faithful to us, He will answer in a way that is for our good!

What if we leaned into that today? What if we turned our cries to God over and over again? What if we waited for Him to move, believing He hears our voice, He meets us with love, and He really does do something with our requests?

- What typically holds you back from "waiting in anticipation" after you present a request to God?

- If praying hasn't been consistent in your life lately, what about prayer has been difficult for you over the past few years?

- How does this prayer here in Psalm 5 encourage you? How does it challenge you?

Lord, I cry out to You today. I lean on Your mercy, and I stop right now to acknowledge that I can't go it alone anymore. I ask You for help, I trust You'll shift my perspective, and I thank You for being the One who can not only move mountains, but can move in me too, shifting my posture from one of worry to one of "waiting in expectation."

DAY
19

God saw all that he had made, and it was very good.

GENESIS 1:31A

It's easy for me to admire a sunset or beautiful flowers or the magnificent way a bird flies through the blue sky with ease and grace. It's easy for me to know that the ocean and the stars and the sun and the mountains are good, but when it comes to looking at myself, this is harder to believe. Some days, it's just so hard to remember that God sees me that way. Do you sometimes forget this too?

This verse in Genesis is such a simple and sweet reminder for me. "God saw all that he had made, and it was very good." *All* of it . . . mankind included. Not some. Not just one or two things. But all. Like an artist stepping back after the last touch to his magnum opus to gaze at it, God looks at the work of His hands, and He's pleased with what He sees.

We are part of His creation, and while I know full well that we're all fallen and that we need rescuing, it's so important for me to remember that before sin ever entered the picture, before we fell, God originally saw us as "very good." I know each of us feels *far* from "good" a lot of days because we live in the days *after* sin entered the world, and we wrestle with it daily. We are fallen people with forgetful hearts, yes, and we aren't perfect yet on this side of heaven, but it's vital to remember two things. One, even though we fail and fall, we are still made in the image of God. We're fearfully and won-derfully made (Ps. 139) to be His image-bearers, reflecting His beauty and creativity and love into the world. And two, even though we are broken, Jesus is an all-sufficient rescuer and He came to restore us and to make us whole. Jesus makes it possible for God to gaze on us once again and say, "very good." That is wonderful news that I so often need to be reminded of!

Let's walk in this truth today together. Right now, let's remember that in God's eyes, we're seen as treasured and beloved and good. Because of Christ, there's simply no other way God can see us. Let's brave the day ahead believing this, and should we start forgetting, let's return to God and ask Him to help us see ourselves through His eyes.

— What's something in creation that you think is very good?

— Is it hard for you to believe that God says you're good? If so, why?

— What environments (or habits in your life) most tempt you to forget that God sees you as "good"?

Father, I'm so thankful for the reminder that when You made the world, You said it was good. Help me remember that even though I've stumbled and fallen, You've done everything necessary to make me "very good" again. On the days I'm tempted to see myself as anything but good, please give me the power to see myself through Your eyes.

DAY
20

He will cover you with his feathers, and under
his wings you will find refuge; his faithfulness
will be your shield and rampart.

PSALM 91:4

Mother or not, every single one of us have children in our life whom we cherish. A niece we love, a grandson we hold dear, a student we've taught with all the energy and care we can muster, a friend's kid who may as well be our own, a Sunday schooler we've invested in for years. No matter what form they take in our life, little ones have a way of lodging themselves in our arms, thoughts, and prayers. We want to pass on the lessons we've learned, share the wisdom we've come across, and impart the specific Bible passages that have impacted our hearts as we journey just a few steps ahead of them.

Psalm 91 is one of those Bible passages for me. Every time my kids have a birthday, I think of it because it is a passage that I pray over their lives again and again. I'm so grateful for the refuge that God has been for me over the years. I'm so grateful that because of what Jesus did on the cross, we can come with all of our mess, with all of our broken pieces, and with all of our fear/shame/doubt/joy/love/longing to the One who loves us most and longs to draw us close and cover us under the shadow of His wing.

What a comfort His faithfulness has been for me, and my prayer is that His faithfulness would be the place my children run for rest, truth, life, and joy. For every day that they feel like the lies are too loud and the storms are too strong, my prayer is that they would find shelter under His wings, and that as they rest there—covered, cared for, completely known *and* loved—they would be restored each time.

I don't know where you are (or where your cherished little one is) on the journey, but I'm thankful that He is our covering today. Thankful it is His faithfulness and not ours that is our shelter. Thankful we don't have to hide or pretend or cover up anything in His sight. We can run to the One who knows and loves us and find our complete covering in Him. Can you imagine what the world might be like if we lived like this were true? Oh how the next generation might be changed if we taught them and *showed* them that it was!

— Who are the cherished children in your life? In what ways are they facing very loud lies? In what ways are they hiding, pretending, or covering up their shame?

— How might you help them find refuge and rest in the wings of God? In what ways might you need to take refuge and find rest in the wings of God?

— What other Bible passages might God be asking you to pray over them and/or yourself?

Father, You know the little faces coming to my mind right now. Please help them run to You in times of trouble or fear, and give them rest, truth, life, and joy under the shelter of Your wings. When they aren't sure how to trust You, help me be a person who shows them what it looks like to trust You for complete covering.

DAY
21

Where can I go from your Spirit? Where can I flee from your presence? If I go up to the heavens, you are there; if I make my bed in the depths, you are there. If I rise on the wings of the dawn, if I settle on the far side of the sea, even there your hand will guide me, your right hand will hold me fast.

PSALM 139:7–10

"I know You love us, God, but surely You can't—or won't—come find me in this situation. I've run too far from You for You to reach me now."

Have you ever had that thought? Have you ever naturally assumed that you've run so far away, God's hand surely wouldn't be willing to uphold you *there*? I have. And you and me, we aren't the only ones. Remember Adam and Eve? They tried to run. Remember Jonah? He tried to run too. Remember Joseph in the Old Testament, in the pit? Surely he thought he had descended far too deep for God to even remember him. Yet in all these cases and more, God found each person and met them exactly where they thought He couldn't. When I'm stuck in those "wanting to run away" moments, I find such comfort in these verses. There is nowhere we can run, nowhere we can hide, that is out of the reach of God's love for us.

I wrote a song inspired by these specific verses on my second EP called "I Can't Outrun Your Love," and I'm just so glad that it's true. God goes with us everywhere. He is with us on our best days and through our worst moments, the ones that we'd never want anyone to know about or see. He is with us, ready to love us, ready to guide us back home to rest in His arms.

Even if the darkness covers me
If I settle on the far side of the sea

No matter what I do, I can't outrun Your love
No, I can't outrun Your love.

If you are running today, or if you feel lost, I hope you'll be reminded that you haven't found the border of where God's love stops. No such border exists, my friend! The truth is that love is right where you are, and I hope, as my friend Katy always says, that "you'll collapse into Jesus' marvelous hands." He's there. Yes, even in *that* place that we assumed He'd never meet us, ready to catch you and me with His strong hands. Let's choose to collapse into them today.

- What situation in your life feels too far away for God's love to find?

- Why do you sometimes assume God wouldn't be willing to guide you in this place?

- What if you believed God's love is right where you are? How would that change your daily perspective and choices?

 Thank You, God, that there's nowhere I can go that is out of Your reach. Thank You for upholding me with Your strong hand no matter where I find myself. Give me the courage today to take Your hand and trust You to lead me home.

If you'd like to sing this psalm with me, it's written into the song called "Where Can I Go" on my album, *All of My Days*.

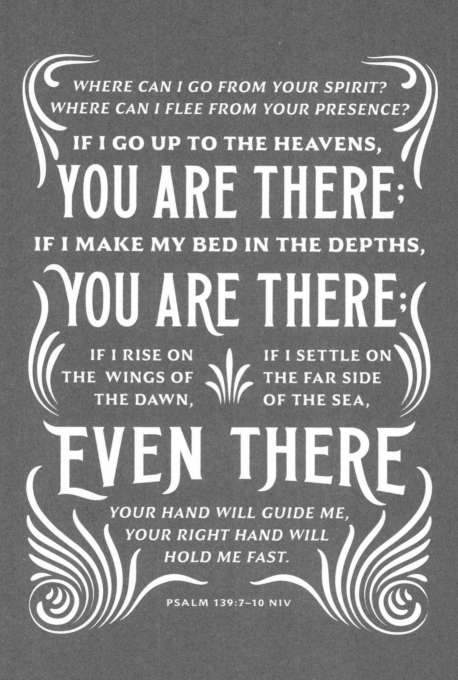

WHERE CAN I GO FROM YOUR SPIRIT?
WHERE CAN I FLEE FROM YOUR PRESENCE?
IF I GO UP TO THE HEAVENS,
YOU ARE THERE;
IF I MAKE MY BED IN THE DEPTHS,
YOU ARE THERE:
IF I RISE ON THE WINGS OF THE DAWN, IF I SETTLE ON THE FAR SIDE OF THE SEA,
EVEN THERE
YOUR HAND WILL GUIDE ME,
YOUR RIGHT HAND WILL
HOLD ME FAST.

PSALM 139:7–10 NIV

DAY
22

Very early in the morning, while it was still
dark, Jesus got up, left the house and went off
to a solitary place, where he prayed.

MARK 1:35

This is what I do every morning: I get up very early in the morning when it is still dark to be alone and to pray.

NOPE. Truth be told, that is not my normal routine, but as I was reading through John recently, I couldn't help but notice that Jesus Himself takes time to go be alone and to pray. I'm not sure how you are feeling as you look at your calendar for this month. Ours is already so *full*, and while it is full of good work, and fun and celebratory things, there is this part of me that is so hungry for space and margin to be alone and to pray. Do you ever feel that way?

I am not always an early riser, but I can tell you this . . . every time I do get up to be alone and to pray, I don't regret it. Every space I carve out to know more of who He is and to sit in His Word, I'm brimming with a lot more life and peace afterward compared to before. I never look back on time that I spent knowing Him more and wish that I had spent that time doing something else.

So today, this verse is set here to help remind our own forgetful and easily distracted hearts to make *room* for Jesus this day and every day. I feel like we will be delighted by what we find in the quiet spaces we carve out during the constant busyness of life.

- Are you an early morning person or a night owl?

- Why do you think Jesus often got up early to be with the Father? How does it encourage you to know that you're not the only one who needs to engage God regularly—that Jesus needed this time with God on a daily basis too?

- What holds you back from rising early in the morning or carving out time in your day to be with Jesus? How can you make more room for Jesus in your schedule this month?

Lord, my life feels so full and busy, but I want to choose the kind of fullness that truly restores my soul instead of depletes it. Please give me the wisdom and creativity and determination to make more room for You today and every day.

DAY 23

So God created mankind in his own image,
in the image of God he created them.

GENESIS 1:27

Have you noticed how angry people can get at each other these days? Whether it is over religion or politics or something else, my heart aches so deeply when I see the world seemingly on fire. So much division. So many insults thrown back and forth. So much hurt.

I love the reminder here in Genesis that we are image-bearers of the Creator of the world. This passage is so healing in a world of hurt, isn't it? Every single person on the planet bears the image and likeness of God Himself. Which means we all—each and every one of us—deserve dignity and honor, no matter our differences. Can you imagine what the world would look like if each of us believed this was true about not only ourselves but our neighbors too?

May I remember this truth as I encounter every man and every woman in my path—that no matter what they believe or how they vote or how they live their life, that they are image-bearers of God. May knowing this grow compassion and patience in me, and also a sense of wonder. And may I remember that I too am an image-bearer of God the next time I start hating on myself.

May we remember that this verse is really and fully and deeply true, and may we treat others (and ourselves!) like it's true too.

— In what situations are you tempted to treat others as less than an image-bearer of God? Why?

- In what situations are you tempted to treat *yourself* as less than His image-bearer? Why?

- Whose eyes are watching your life right now? Who might learn how to treat other people by the way you treat others? How does this encourage or challenge you?

- How could your family and neighborhood and church look different if you lived like this verse was true with every person you encounter?

Oh Lord, would You shape my heart to look more and more like Yours? Would You give me eyes to see the dignity and value of every soul I come across in this life? Please help me stand in wonder once again at the way You've made every human being in Your image and for Your glory.

DAY
24

Finally, be strong in the Lord and in his mighty power.
Put on the full armor of God, so that you can take your
stand against the devil's schemes. For our struggle is not
against flesh and blood, but against the rulers, against
the authorities, against the powers of this dark world
and against the spiritual forces of evil in the heavenly
realms. Therefore put on the full armor of God, so that
when the day of evil comes, you may be able to stand your
ground, and after you have done everything, to stand.

Stand firm then, with the belt of truth buckled around
your waist, with the breastplate of righteousness in
place, and with your feet fitted with the readiness that
comes from the gospel of peace. In addition to all this,
take up the shield of faith, with which you can extinguish
all the flaming arrows of the evil one. Take the helmet of
salvation and the sword of the Spirit, which is the word
of God. And pray in the Spirit on all occasions with all
kinds of prayers and requests. With this in mind, be alert
and always keep on praying for all the Lord's people.

EPHESIANS 6:10–18

Can you remember a time when you felt too weary to keep
fighting the good fight against the constant attack of the enemy? Or
maybe even too tired to even get out of bed in the morning? If you're
anything like me, there are seasons you've faced where the answer
is yes and yes.

This life can beat us down, and I think that's why I love this instruction from God's Word. It doesn't say, "Be stronger" or "do better" or "get it together already." Instead, it points us to the source of all strength: the Lord.

These verses tell us to rest in His mighty arms and to stand on His strength when we might not have any left. How can we be strong on the days we feel so done or tired? We can anchor ourselves in the Lord and His mighty power. If you're wondering how to do this today, to root yourself in His strength, I would encourage you to focus in on the second half of this passage from Ephesians 6:10–18. It lays out many of the tools that help us to stand firm and to rely on the sure and steady strength of the Lord as we fight against the darkness.

Weary as we may be, instead of a guilt trip, God kindly gives us exactly what we need to keep fighting. He fills our tired arms with strength, and helps train them to fight using His power, not our own. We raise our hands up in emptiness and He fills them with *help*—with heavenly equipment to protect us and arm us for the fight at hand. What grace!

Today, let's rest in His great strength and use the armor He's given us to push back against the enemy, and anything else that might keep us from Him.

— What makes you want to give up the good fight? Why?

— How have you been running away from the mighty power of God in this season instead of toward it?

— How are the tools here in Ephesians 6 different from the tools you typically use to fight your battles? How are they better?

Lord, thank You for giving me a place to run when I'm weak—your mighty arms. Give me the courage to fight the battles I face with the tools You've given me instead of in my own power. Help me stand firm in Your strength today.

Therefore, as God's chosen people, holy and dearly loved,
clothe yourselves with compassion, kindness, humility,
gentleness and patience. Bear with each other and forgive
one another if any of you has a grievance against someone.
Forgive as the Lord forgave you. And over all these virtues
put on love, which binds them all together in perfect unity.

COLOSSIANS 3:12–14

This verse is always a wonderful one to think on, but I find that it comes to my mind most often as I get dressed. So many times, when I need to prepare myself for an outing or just for the day, I'm running around trying to figure out what to wear. I can still remember when I was a few days away from welcoming our third kid into the world, most things didn't *fit at all*, so the whole getting dressed thing could get complicated. Pregnant or not, the experience of getting ready can get us all in a tizzy at some point.

But what if instead of rushing about in a flurry of worry about what clothes to wear, I focused on clothing my spirit with compassion, kindness, humility, gentleness, and patience? What if I stopped to remember the forgiveness that God has lavished upon me and making sure to forgive those who have hurt me? What if before I put on any outfit, I make sure to put on *love*? What if I began the getting-ready process by simply remembering that I am dearly loved by the God of the universe, and because of that, I can love those around me (even when they are difficult and hard to love)?

I'm not knocking cute outfits here, and I'm not saying it's wrong for us to think about what we're going to wear for a certain occasion or simply for an ordinary day. But I'm pretty sure my heart and my family and all of the people I encounter every day would be better off if I focused first on clothing myself with compassion, kindness, humility, gentleness, and patience . . . putting on *love* first. I can only imagine how different my life would look if, when I needed to throw together an outfit, I prepared my inner person as much as I prepared my outer person! Let's try this together today—let's put on love above all else, and watch how God uses it for His glory and our good.

— In the moments when you need to get yourself ready, how much time do you spend figuring out what to wear?

— What would it look like to spend as much time clothing your inner self as you do clothing your outer self? How might this change a typical day for you?

— Write this verse out in your own words, and see what God might teach you in the process.

◖ Father, help me put on love today before I put on anything else. Teach me what compassion, kindness, humility, gentleness, patience, and forgiveness look like when they are worn well—and help others see these things as evidence of Your work and love as I aim to walk in Your ways throughout the day.

"Do not let your hearts be troubled.
Trust in God; trust also in me."

JOHN 14:1

Are you harboring some sort of trouble today? Does your heart accumulate worries as fast as mine does? Because I can promise you this, burdens tend to pile on fast over here in my heart. That is why I love this verse. It is so simple, and it whispers the direction that I can take my worry . . . straight to Jesus. He is the kindest person I've ever known.

Don't you love that Jesus' answer for feeling troubled is to *trust*? Goodness knows I do. Of all the answers for worry He could give us, He tells us to simply trust Him. Why? Because as this verse hints at, He's not just a kind friend. He's also *God*. This means He's the most trustworthy and powerful place to take our troubles! In this verse, Jesus is helping us see that trusting Him with something is the equivalent of trusting God with it. No other friend can tell us that! This trust is easier said than done, of course, but every time I lift my eyes from the circumstance that is troubling me to the One who can calm troubled waters and troubled hearts, I experience peace.

Now, don't get me wrong. It's not that trusting Jesus waves a magic wand over the craziness of life swirling all around me, making it disappear. The real miracle is not that He makes the painful or crazy situations different, but that He makes *me* different. As I choose to trust Him even in circumstances I can't understand, He takes my worry, and in exchange, He gives me the reminder that because He's God, He can handle it. I pray today that we will choose to let trust rather than trouble rule in our hearts. Praying that we will listen to the kind whisper in this verse, and take our troubles to only the One who can give us peace in return.

— What specific troubles are plaguing your heart today?

— How do you typically handle worries as they accumulate throughout your day? Do you mentally fixate on them? Shove them down emotionally? Offload them to someone in particular? Run to a bad habit?

— Why is Jesus a trustworthy source to run to with your troubles? How is He uniquely qualified to help you?

🔥 Jesus, help me trust You in this moment! My worries are accumulating, and I feel the temptation to keep them from You, to shoulder them myself. Help me give my troubles to You, in the knowledge that You are God, which means You're the safest and strongest person to handle them.

DAY
27

Look to the Lᴏʀᴅ and his strength;
seek his face always.

PSALM 105:4

Not sure how you have been lately, but I recently came through a four-day stint of feeling *really* sick! I had all the upper respiratory junk and with twenty shows on the books, I felt totally bummed and overwhelmed because it's really hard to sing when you are sick like that. Cue all the vitamin C and sleep and steam showers and essential oils and hot tea and Sudafed, and thank *goodness* I started feeling better!

If you're sick today, I'm so sorry, and I hope you get better soon. At the same time, something struck me when was in the middle of feeling so bad. It is times like these, when I feel so sick and so weak, that I tend to really cry out to the Lord. Is that true for you too?

I was literally asking God for strength . . . for strength to play my guitar, for strength to get up early to catch my early morning flight, for strength to make it through each song at my shows, for strength to do all the momma things when I got back home. Don't get me wrong. I rested lots too, but there is something beautiful about being very aware of your weakness and then very aware of God helping you in the midst of that weak place.

This verse in Psalm 105 was a reminder for me during those sick days that no matter how we are feeling, we always have the opportunity to look to the Lord and His strength. This verse feels like a directive to "seek His face always"; but more than that, it feels like an invitation to us. I've never regretted spending time to seek God's face. I've never regretted asking Him for strength rather than trying to muster it up myself either, and I am amazed at how something in my heart and soul changes—even during seasons of feeling very weak—when I simply shift my gaze from my circumstances to God's face. I suppose it's one of those reminders that whatever we are facing, He wants us to seek His face and find His strength, and I don't know about you, but I'm so grateful for that reminder on sick days and healthy days alike!

- Can you remember a time you felt really sick? What was that like?

- How did your spiritual posture toward God change during that time?

- How did God help you in the midst of that experience? How might you take the lessons you learned in that season into your "healthy" days?

Lord, help me look to You for my strength today instead of trying to muster it up on my own. Empower me to remember that through sick and healthy days alike, I am not alone, and You delight in strengthening me in all my weak places.

DAY
28

The LORD will fulfill his purpose for me; your love, O LORD,
endures forever—do not abandon the works of your hands.

PSALM 138:8

I love David, the author of many of the Psalms. I love how he closes Psalm 138. He reminds his soul that the Lord *will* be faithful! What a relief, y'all! God, who called us and drew us to Himself, is faithful and will continue to be faithful toward His purposes for us. After all, His love "endures forever."

But then, as certain as these statements of God's faithfulness sound, David prays—"do not abandon the work of your hands." Do you feel like this some days? You are certain of who God is and of how He loves faithfully, but then you wonder if that love will be applied to you and the messes you make with your heart and your choices? I have *been* there, and I love how David is always trying to boss his soul around, reminding himself of what is true, and yet, in the same breath, he isn't scared to be honest with God and to direct his hurt, his fear, his doubt, and his needs to the One whose love endures forever. In other words, David has shown me that prayer makes room for both *remembrance* (declaring what is true) and *honesty* (declaring how we are actually feeling about that truth in the moment), which is so freeing, isn't it? May we be like that, reminding ourselves of what is true, *and* coming as we are—with all of our concerns and questions.

God can handle us, and He loves it when we come to Him. He's not scared or overwhelmed by our mess, and He doesn't abandon the work of His hands. The God whose love lasts for all eternity WILL fulfill His purpose for us. What if we followed the way David models both remembrance and honesty over and over again throughout the Psalms? May we do it! May we continue to approach God with all the real stuff going on in our heart, and then fight to remember the truth that He won't ever give up on His commitment to us.

- Do you ever assume God can't handle your honest prayers? Why or why not?

- Do your prayers lean more toward *remembrance* or *honesty*? How might your relationship with the Lord change for the better if you chose to lean into both of these things?

- Where in your life do you feel like God may have forgotten to fulfill His purposes for you? Do you draw near to Him when you feel this way? If not, why?

Lord, help me learn to come to You like Your Word says I can. Help me be faithful enough to cling to the truth that You will never abandon Your work in my life, and at the same time, help me be honest enough to run to You for help in the moments that I'm tempted to believe otherwise. Give me the strength to remember what's true, and give me the courage to come as I am.

DAY
29

Jesus answered her, "If you knew the gift of God and
who it is that asks you for a drink, you would have asked
him and he would have given you living water."

JOHN 4:10

This encounter that Jesus has with the Samaritan woman at the well is one of my favorite scenes in the Bible. You know what stands out to me? I love that Jesus continually *sees* people. I love that in a culture where women were not seen or valued much at all, Jesus takes the time to interact with this woman and her story.

And not only that, He reveals to her the truth. The truth about her own broken story, and the beautiful truth of what He came to do: to give us living water, to satisfy our weary and thirsty souls with His love. We go to other "wells," thinking they will fill us . . . and they might—for a short while. But eventually those wells run dry. Here, we see that Jesus is the only One who can fill us all the way up to the point of overflow. He doesn't run dry or run out on us. And that goes for even the lowliest of us. *Especially* the lowliest of us.

At the time I originally wrote these words, it was International Women's Day, and I was celebrating the beauty and strength in women. This passage came to my mind, and I celebrated that Jesus really saw and engaged with women in a radical way during His time here. They may have been lowly in their culture, but they mattered to Him. He drew near, offering to be a better well than they had ever drawn from. He does the same today for you and for me. He sees us, and just like the woman at the well, He sees us fully, all of our mistakes, all of our efforts to try to satisfy the thirst in our souls with other things besides Him, and yet . . . He offers us living water anyway!

What a joy to know that we are all fully *seen* and by the God who made us. Aren't you? Oh Lord, help us say yes to Your invitation to be filled up by Your living water today to the point of overflow.

- In what ways do you feel unseen by others in your daily tasks, work, or life?

- How does it feel to know Jesus sees you and draws near today?

- What "thirst" do you sense most in your soul these days? What "wells" do you typically draw from to quench this thirst?

- In what specific ways is Jesus a better satisfier of this thirst?

Jesus, thank You that You see me fully and offer to fill me up fully with Your living water. Would You continue to help me return to You if I've drawn from other wells, and would You quench my thirst today?

Being confident of this, that he who began
a good work in you will carry it on to
completion until the day of Christ Jesus.

PHILIPPIANS 1:6

Have you ever seen a house on the side of the road that was left unfinished? Like the workers began the project, but maybe the resources ran out to see it through, and they all abandoned the home? I've seen one of those before. The house just sits there, day after day, year after year, stuck in that same half-done place with no hope of being fully completed.

Maybe, like that house, you feel stuck today. Maybe you feel half-done in your attempts to be like Jesus in this world. Maybe you feel abandoned, or maybe you wish you could be a little farther along than you are. *So* often, I do too. I get discouraged because I think I'll have learned something, and then I forget. I fall. I fail.

I'm so grateful for this promise from Philippians today, for the precious reminder that God *will* carry on the good work He started in us. We are works-in-progress on a journey of being made more and more like Him. So grateful He doesn't leave the work to someone else who might give up or abandon it or run out of resources. No, *He* is the one who finishes the good work. It's not up to us, but man oh man, this truth makes me want to repent when I get things wrong, return to Him, and to remember that every mistake I make can be a step toward Him reminding me of His mercy and that He is not finished with me yet!

Here's our good news today, my friend: we get to rest in the patient hands of the One who loves us most. We may be unfinished, but we aren't stuck. We aren't abandoned. He has not run out of resources in His work of restoration. Day after day, year after year,

He's *still* showing up. He's *still* working and changing us. And He *will* finish His work. God finishes whatever work He starts, including you and me—He will never stop renewing and remaking us!

- In what ways do you feel stuck in your spiritual journey?

- When you sense that you are "unfinished," what do you typically do to try and fix yourself up?

- How does this verse soothe your fears and worries? How does it challenge your attempts to do the work of restoration all by yourself?

- Look back on your life and write something down that you have seen God change in your heart over the years.

- How does it encourage you to know that He has already been at work and that He will continue that kind of good work in you?

Lord, thank You for being a God who always completes what He starts! In the moments I feel stuck or unfinished, help me return to the truth that You are not done with me yet, and that You'll never give up on Your commitment to make me more like You.

DAY
31

My flesh and my heart may fail, but God is the
strength of my heart and my portion forever.

PSALM 73:26

This is one of the first verses I ever memorized, and I can't quit it. I love that it openly acknowledges that we may fail. I don't know about you, but I fail *all* the time, and it is here in our failures and mistakes that the two words "but God" come crashing into all of our "not enough."

I'm so grateful that God promises to be our strength and our portion, even when we fail. Grace isn't something we earn; it's a gift we receive. It's a gift I'm all the more grateful for when I come to the end of myself and the end of my resources only to find that God is my portion.

If you've ever heard my song "My Portion and My Strength," this is the verse that song was inspired by.

Help me to stand on the promise that
You are holding my right hand
Help me to know, that even when I lose my grip You won't let go
Help me believe, that You will be my portion and my strength.

More than a song, this is a prayer I'll continue to pray all my days—that God would help me believe even in my stumbling, that He will be my portion and my strength. This is true for me and for you. For all of us who call on His name.

When the lies close in and tell us that our "not enough" will remain as it is, lacking and deficient, here's the truth that both of us can fight with: Christ has already covered our lack with His "more than enough." He's filled our holes, our mistakes, and our failures with His abundant righteousness and grace, and He does this freely as a gift! Not because we've earned it. Not because we've begged hard enough or because we deserve it. He does this because He chose to set His love on us. He does this because He wants to cover our failures, and He has. That is some good news, friends.

- Where do you feel like you're failing right now?
- How does the lie that "it's all on me to be enough" play out in your life?
- In what areas of your life is God showing you that He doesn't want you to try to earn grace, and that He wants to be your portion and strength?

Jesus, help me believe that even in my biggest mistakes, You will be my portion and my strength. Give me power to fight the lie that You have left me in my failure, and grant me faith to believe that Your "more than enough" always covers my "not enough."

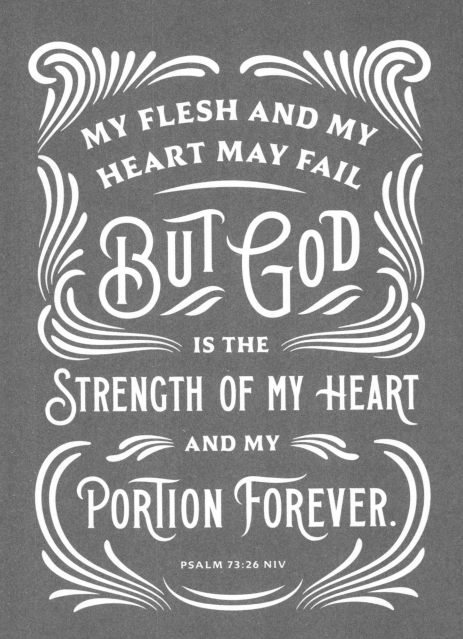

MY FLESH AND MY HEART MAY FAIL BUT GOD IS THE STRENGTH OF MY HEART AND MY PORTION FOREVER.

PSALM 73:26 NIV

DAY
32

Consequently, you are no longer foreigners
and strangers, but fellow citizens with God's
people and also members of his household.

EPHESIANS 2:19

Have you ever been so close to someone that you felt like a member of their family? Growing up, I can remember parents of a few close friends introducing me, saying something to the tune of, "Oh, and this is Ellie, she's like a daughter to us! She may as well be part of our household!"

I'm reminded of those memories when I look at this verse in Ephesians. It tells us we are not a random person on the street to God, but part of His household. We may once have been strangers outside His family, but because of Christ, now we're not. Now we're in the family, joining in on the fun and the festivities and the favor that comes with having a warm and loving parent.

I also can't help but notice the communal nature of this verse— we're "fellow" family members with others who know God as Father too. And I suppose that makes sense; after all, no household can run with only one person trying to do it all. When we look back on what households were like back in the days Ephesians was written, we remember that it took *a lot* of people to pull it off. These weren't nuclear families of four or five; no, households included dozens and dozens of people! The cooks and the gardeners and the door keepers and the business experts—they were all considered part of the family. Everyone had a part to play, a role in the household that mattered. And here in Ephesians, we're told that we get to be part of God's household—we've all got a unique contribution to make, and together, we help it run well for outsiders to come in out of the storm and find it vibrant and refreshing.

Lies may rush in, telling us there's nowhere we belong, but God's Word flies in the face of all that and shows us the truth. If you are struggling to feel like you have a place in this world today, be encouraged: you're part of God's household. You have a unique place there, your part in His family matters dearly to Him, and you have "fellow" brothers and sisters who are standing right beside you.

- What does "household" mean to you? What was yours like growing up?

- How is God's household different than the one you grew up in?

- What unique contribution has God equipped you to make in His household? If you don't feel like you belong to any "household" of sorts, spend some time today to ask the Lord to show you where you might show up and be a part of a living and vibrant community of other believers.

Father, thank You for bringing me into Your big, beautiful family! When I'm tempted to believe that I don't have a place to belong, help me remember I have a unique contribution to make in Your household, and that You've given me brothers and sisters to belong with, as well.

DAY
33

May the words of my mouth and the meditation
of my heart be acceptable in Your sight,
Lord, my rock and my Redeemer.

PSALM 19:14 NASB

When my mom was in middle school, she found herself in the midst of a group of girls gossiping in the hall (sound familiar?). In the middle of this conversation, one of those girls quietly walked away. My mom followed her and asked, "Was that one of your friends that they were talking about?" The girl responded, "Oh no, but I just love Jesus and I don't think that it's very loving to talk about anyone behind their back, but I knew that I would if I kept standing there. I also didn't want to preach at anyone, so I just decided that the most loving thing to do was to walk away." My mom was dumbfounded. She didn't grow up in the church and had only really ever been to church on holidays like Easter or Christmas. She says now that she had two thoughts after that interaction: The first was, "Who is this Jesus guy? I haven't ever heard anyone talk about Him like that before." The second was, "Will you be my new best friend because that was such a loving way to handle that situation and you seem awesome."

My mom started to hang out with this new friend and her amazing family, and Mom describes it like this: "I ended up encountering the Living God, and it was like my world went from black and white to 3D and color!" My mom met the Lord, and her entire family ended up encountering the Living God as well all because of one middle school girl and the words that she did not say.

I *love* this verse from Psalm 19 because it reminds me that our words are powerful. They have the power to bring about life and light, and they have the power to bring about the opposite of that. That goes for the words we speak to others, but also for the words we speak over ourselves.

When I think about the "meditations of my heart," these are the things that I find my mind circling around and around again . . . that could be something lovely and beautiful like God's Word or His character, or it could be a conflict I'm facing, a worry I can't seem to shake, or wondering what others are thinking of me, but I love that this verse points us to steadying our minds and our vision on what is beautiful and true. This verse and my mom's story are powerful reminders to me to pray this beautiful prayer throughout all of my days: "May the words of my mouth and the meditation of my heart be acceptable in Your sight."

My dad actually wrote this psalm into a song in the '70s. I sang it *all* the time walking around my college campus, and I sing it to this day; a hummed prayer that God would help me use the words of my mouth to bring about light and life is just the kind of thing I want stuck in my head and my heart.

— Describe a time you were impacted by the power of someone's words. This could be positive or negative.

— What does your heart tend to meditate on throughout the day?

— How might you speak life and light into your own heart or into someone else's life today?

— Write this verse out and put it somewhere around your house that you will see before you walk out the door. What would it look like to pray through this verse before you go to work, engage with your family, or have conversation with friends?

Lord, help me to be the kind of person who speaks life into my own heart and into the world around me. Help me to hold my tongue when I need to, and to speak words of truth and grace when I need to. May both the words in my mouth and the meditations of my heart bring You glory.

DAY
34

Shout for joy to the LORD, all the earth. Worship
the LORD with gladness; come before him with joyful
songs. . . . For the LORD is good and his love endures forever;
his faithfulness continues through all generations.

PSALM 100:1–2, 5

"For the LORD is good."
"His love endures forever."
"His faithfulness continues through all generations."

I don't know what your favorite phrases in this passage are, but these three statements give me such hope. God is good and trustworthy. Even when our circumstances are hard, even when we are in a season of longing or loss, His goodness doesn't change. God's love endures, it *never* tires out.

My kids *love* the song "One Thing Remains," and I can't tell you how sweet it is to hear them belt these lyrics out in the car: "Your love never fails, it never gives up, it never runs out on me." I love hearing them sing of God's enduring love, because it's one of the truest things I've experienced in my life. Endurance means making it through to the other side, no matter how strong the obstacle or resistance. When I think of the deepest loss and longing I feel in life, or the places where I still have questions and doubts, this verse helps me realize that God's love endures through all that. It pushes through all that resistance, making its way past these things I consider obstacles, because it's stronger than all those things. God's love will always meet me on the other side. It won't ever tire out; it endures!

And then, as I hear my children sing this truth, I'm reminded of the last part of this verse from Psalm 100, "His faithfulness continues through all generations." He doesn't change, and even though I know

I will fall short as a parent (though it's the *last* thing I ever want to do), I'm reminded that God is a *good* and *loving* Father who will be faithful to me and who will be faithful to my kids and their kids too, no matter what.

So grateful for this simple and beautiful truth and for the way it gives us good reason to *shout* and to *rejoice* with our voices and with our very lives. Let's remember and rejoice today that God is good, that His love sees us through no matter what, and that His faithfulness and love endure forever, pushing past even our lives and on down the line, into the lives of those who come after us, like a force that can't be stopped.

— Do you ever think God's love for you won't be able to endure? Why?

— How does it make you feel to know God's faithfulness is not exhausted by your current moment or even your lifetime, but has the power to keep pouring out?

— What might "worshiping the Lord with gladness" look like in your life today in light of the truth in this verse?

Father, help me remember You are good. Open my eyes to just how much Your love endures in my life, no matter what. When I'm tempted to assume Your goodness, faithfulness, and love are limited, help me return to this truth in Your Word, and strengthen me to believe that it's true.

"Peace I leave with you; my peace I give you. I
do not give as the world gives. Do not let your
hearts be troubled and do not be afraid."

JOHN 14:27

I'll never forget singing this verse out over and over again in the parking lot of Vanderbilt Children's Hospital. My friend's son was not doing well. He had a really bad infection, and the doctors thought it might be his last day here on earth. The doctors told our friends to prepare to say goodbye to their son. It was devastating. This was last year during Covid, and while we all wanted to be in the hospital to surround and support and pray for this precious family, we simply couldn't be, so a team of friends and family circled up socially distanced in the parking garage to pray and to sing over this precious boy and his family.

I had been memorizing this verse at the time, and as we were praying, I simply started singing it over and over again. It felt impossible to follow this instruction from God's Word: "Do not let your hearts be troubled and do not be afraid."

How on earth were we supposed to not let our hearts be afraid and troubled when our dear friends were about to lose their son? But as I sang this verse, it echoed through that empty parking garage reminding me that His voice has echoed through an empty grave before. As I heard other voices of friends sing this verse with me, it reminded me that even in hospital rooms when we are given a dire diagnosis, even when the threat of our last breath here on earth is present, there is a presence of LOVE that is always with us. Jesus doesn't give as the world gives. His gift of love to the world is a love that beats death, and as we sang this promise in that deeply troubled place, we began to experience God's peace, even in the face of impossibly sorrowful circumstances.

The crazy part of this story? That precious little boy lived! He is thriving. And while I know full well that not every sick little child is healed on this side of glory, I also know that ultimately, the gift that Jesus gives that no one else can give is life eternal. I'm so grateful for that hope, but also, for those of us mourning the loss of a child or a parent or a friend or a life, I'm grateful for the peace Jesus offers us even in the face of our deepest losses, troubles, and fears.

This verse helps me understand that if we can shift our focus from our fears to His face, our hearts will encounter a Love that runs deeper than all of our troubles. It's not that the fear or trouble isn't a real thing; it's that it's getting replaced by the greater and stronger things of God.

Jesus offers us a peace that is available at all times, so let's trust Him to help us take hold of the peace He gives us freely, allowing it to change the way we walk through fear and trouble.

- If you made a list of the fears you're facing today in particular, what would be on that list?

- If you made a list of truths about God that bring calmness and peace to your soul, what would be on that list?

- Take a moment to switch lists right now before the Lord—giving God the ones on the "fear" list and taking for yourself the ones on the "peace" list.

🔥 Jesus, thank You for leaving us Your presence and peace to take hold of even as we face trouble. Help me experience and rest in Your peace today, even in the middle of all my troubles and fears.

For if we have been united with him in a death like his,
we will certainly also be united with him in a resurrection
like his. For we know that our old self was crucified with
him so that the body ruled by sin might be done away
with, that we should no longer be slaves to sin— because
anyone who has died has been set free from sin.

Now if we died with Christ, we believe that we will also
live with him. For we know that since Christ was raised
from the dead, he cannot die again; death no longer
has mastery over him. The death he died, he died to
sin once for all; but the life he lives, he lives to God.

In the same way, count yourselves dead to sin but alive
to God in Christ Jesus. Therefore do not let sin reign in
your mortal body so that you obey its evil desires. Do
not offer any part of yourself to sin as an instrument
of wickedness, but rather offer yourselves to God as
those who have been brought from death to life; and
offer every part of yourself to him as an instrument of
righteousness. For sin shall no longer be your master,
because you are not under the law, but under grace.

ROMANS 6:5–14

I spent a *lot* of years controlled by what other people thought
of me. I would work myself up into a tizzy, worried about what
others might assume about me if I didn't live my life perfectly. I was

dominated by the false idea that my worth came from whether or not others approved of me. I did not live free. I might have *looked* like I had a full and wonderful life in which I was making good decisions and growing in my faith, but truly? I was living a life of fear, worried that if I didn't get life exactly right, I would be rejected by others and by God. I wasn't just struggling with needing approval from others, I was being mastered by it.

I once heard it said that we're all mastered by something. And, goodness, if I get a choice on what that something could be, I want it to be the love of God. As I've done the daily, hard work of choosing that path, the Lord has been so kind to not leave me in my approval issues, but to free me up to rest in all He has done for us. I'm so grateful, and I'm undone that He's liberated me from an existence where sin was my master. I don't always get it right, and I feel the pull back toward needing approval sometimes, but I'm awestruck that I am no longer held down underneath the weight of all that guilt, but have the option to live *free* under grace.

I want to post all the praise hands emojis for the beautiful truth this promise from Romans carries, because it reminds me of the ways Jesus has freed us. On the days we forget, or feel the pull back toward sin, it reminds us that we get to step away from all of that and into His grace and mercy as we offer ourselves to Him day by day. We no longer have to be defined by that same old struggle, but by the extravagant love God demonstrated for us on the cross. And when we are marked by that kind of love, it is a beautiful thing because we come alive. Alive to God in Christ Jesus. Alive to be the accepted, beloved, covered, and free image-bearer that we were intended to be!

If you want a beautiful picture of the life Jesus lived so that we wouldn't have to be stuck in our sin, read through Romans 6:5–14 again today. Let's just keep reading it over and over again. And then let's walk in the promises it speaks over us and the freedom it offers us today and every day.

- Do you typically define yourself by your struggles or by God's extravagant love for you?

- What were you once mastered by before coming to know Jesus? In what ways do you sometimes forget you do not have to be mastered by those things anymore?

- What do you think a life lived totally "under grace" looks like? What changes would need to take place in your life in order to live this way? How might God be helping you live freer now than you ever have?

God, thank You for calling me out of the things that once mastered me, into Your restorative and redeeming love. Thank You for freeing me into a life of resting and rejoicing in what You've done for me. When I start to forget, please help me remember that guilt and shame and sin does not define me any longer, but instead, Your love, grace, and mercy.

DAY
37

Blessed are those who have learned to acclaim you,
who walk in the light of your presence, LORD.

PSALM 89:15

To acclaim something or someone, means to praise enthusiastically and publicly. What are you quick to acclaim? I'm real quick to tell someone that they look great if I like their outfit, for example. Or when I walk into a friend's home that is decorated beautifully, when I see my kids do something bravely, or when I eat a great meal . . . I am quick to acclaim these sorts of things. I don't think this verse is saying that those things are wrong, but it does point out that those who learn to praise the Lord enthusiastically and publicly will be blessed.

I started to wonder why that is . . . why does learning to acclaim the Lord turn around and bless us? I honestly think it must be good for us, because as followers of Jesus, our work is to *remember*, and when we praise God for who He is and for all He's done for us, our memories are jolted into recounting His goodness and grace and power and tenderness and strength. For me, the work of acclaiming/ remembering frees me up to come walk in the light of God's presence.

If I don't first remember how good and full of mercy God is, I am often prone to feeling like I need to pull it all together before I come to Him. But God's presence isn't like that. At least it's not supposed to be. We're supposed to feel the freedom to come before Him as we are—no "pulling ourselves together" required.

I'm always moved by what happens to my soul when I remember this truth and turn my real self—my problems, my insecurities, my needs, my victories, my losses, my pain, my sorrow, and my joy— toward the Lord. As I bring all of it into the light of His presence, I am relieved to find a Companion, a Rescuer, and a Shepherd who leads me beside quiet waters.

We are always blessed when we recount the ways He has loved us. We are always given grace when we come to Him as we are without pretense. We are always accepted and loved when we walk in the light of God's presence.

- Who or what are you quick to acclaim?
- Why do you sometimes try to clean yourself up before entering God's presence?
- How has Jesus helped you enter into the light of God's presence without fear?
- What do you need to lay before God's presence today? How can you turn your full self toward Him?

Father, help me to learn to acclaim You more and more to remind my forgetful heart of Your goodness and love. Instead of pulling it together before I come to You, help me to enter Your presence without fear, forever walking in Your light.

. . . the Spirit helps us in our weakness. For we do not
know what to pray for as we ought, but the Spirit himself
intercedes for us with groanings too deep for words.

ROMANS 8:26 ESV

I don't know about you, but I always fall into thinking that God
is upset with me in the moments I don't know what to do, or I'm too
tired to even ask Him how to handle something. I often think I have to
muster up the strength to get through this life all by myself.

But this verse in Romans 8 flies in the face of all that, doesn't it?
God's Spirit "helps us in our weakness." Not points the finger at us.
Not judges us. Not condemns us. *Helps* us. What a wonderful promise
that shows us what our God is like—He's both kind to want to help us
and mighty to actually be able to!

And it gets better. The Holy Spirit does not only help us in our
weakness if we cry out with all the right words. No. The Spirit cries
out *for* us when we don't know what to say! When we feel too weak
to even come up with an intelligible prayer, the Spirit is already there,
interceding for us to the Father, with groanings "too deep for words."
How beautiful is that? The Holy Spirit is interceding for you and for
me before God the Father right now, helping us along, even when we
feel helpless and hopeless.

I need that reminder of God's grace and love and help today.
Let's face whatever comes our way this week knowing that this is
the kind of God we serve—a Spirit who helps us in our weakness and
prays for us too!

- How do you typically assume God responds to you when you don't know what to do, or when you feel weak? How does it feel to know that God's response is *help*, and that the Holy Spirit is interceding for you right now?

- If this is what God's Spirit does in response to our weakness, what should we do in response to the weaknesses of those around us?

- What situation in your life do you not have words for right now? How can you rest in this promise from God's Word in that speechless place?

Thank You, God, that Your response to my weakness is to send help. Thank You that when I don't have the words to pray, the Spirit intercedes with groanings too deep for words. Help me to comfort others with the comfort I've received from You, and open my eyes to how I might intercede and show up for others when they are feeling weak.

"This is my command: Love each other."

JOHN 15:17

Not too long ago, we spent two weeks as a family at a Young Life camp in Colorado, and we loved every minute of being there. It's beautiful. It's fun. And if you know our family at all, you know that it's not just a random camp for us. It's a ministry God has deeply embedded in our own stories.

A few people asked me why we pause our busy schedule to come volunteer at camp, and this verse is why. Young Life is all about simply following that command: *love each other*. If you aren't familiar with it, Young Life is a para-church organization that believes all kids everywhere deserve a chance to hear the gospel in a way that they can understand it. Their method? Loving people.

Let's imagine you're a middle school, high school, or college kid. The volunteer leaders in Young Life show the love of Jesus by simply showing up in your life. Leaders know your name, go to your games and performances, have lunch with you at school, mentor you, hang out with you, and answer your calls and texts, even the ones you send at 2:00 a.m. They offer meetings every week where they play games and sing and present the gospel, and every kid is invited to come to camp in the summer for "the best week of their life," where they can come as they are and hear a clear presentation of the gospel in a beautiful place while having an absolute blast. No matter how kids respond to this gospel message, Young Life leaders simply continue to show up and be present in each kid's life.

Every time I go to Young Life camp, I'm reminded that it's all about loving each other, showing up for each other, and sharing the love of God with a broken and weary world. It's not easy, but it is pretty simple, and I'm always grateful for the reminder of what love looks like on full display. You see it everywhere at camp, because every leader and staff person and volunteer has the singular focus of showing up for kids, loving them well, and saying "follow me as I follow Jesus." I tend to leave Young Life camp remembering that this kind of love doesn't have to stay at camp, or within a certain ministry. It's the model Jesus lived out for us. It should be the way we all seek to treat each other. What if we did? What if our approach to life was simply showing up and loving people well?

- What friend, mentor, ministry, or event most helped you understand what love truly looked like?

- Why do you think we often forget the simple command to love each other? What gets in the way?

- I'll never forget the day an amazing Young Life staff woman, Eve, came up to me at camp and said, "Can we meet up in Nashville from time to time so I can just pour Jesus into you?" Who might the Lord be calling you to "pour Jesus into" right now?

Lord, help me to remember that You intended our lives to be all about pouring out the love You lavish on us. Help me see the ways You might have me show up for other people this week, and give me the strength to love them well.

And we boast in the hope of the glory of God. Not only
so, but we also glory in our sufferings, because we know
that suffering produces perseverance; perseverance,
character; and character, hope. And hope does not put us
to shame, because God's love has been poured out into our
hearts through the Holy Spirit, who has been given to us.

ROMANS 5:2–5

When I was younger, I never would have said that I "gloried" in
my suffering. To *glory* means to "take great pride or pleasure in." I
don't know what your personality type is, but mine is one that hates
pain more than most, and so . . . I avoid it at all cost, which means that
this is not one of those verses I naturally gravitate toward.

But regardless of my personality type or preferences, the truth is
that this is a broken world, and pain comes to all of us in one way or
another. In a fallen world, pain and suffering is universal. We all know
what it is to hurt. But Romans 5 tells us something so amazing: all
that difficulty serves a purpose. Like an athlete trying to train, each
moment that feels so painful actually helps us get stronger. As we
go through more and more moments of strain, our tolerance starts
to increase, and we learn to persevere through the next moment of
difficulty instead of being thrown down by it. And then, after whole
seasons of perseverance, we turn around and realize we have devel-
oped Christlike character, for He was the most perseverant man on
the planet! And what's more, as our character grows, so does our
hope.

Speaking of hope, I'm so thankful for the perseverance, character,
and hope that suffering has produced in my life, but I'm also deeply
grateful that we don't have some flimsy or feel-good version of hope.
Our hope "does not put us to shame" because we have a hope that is

grounded in an empty grave. Death doesn't have the last say. We can "glory" in our suffering because we know that suffering is never the end, and we have the same power that raised Jesus from the dead living inside us! Y'all. That is CRAZY. What a comfort. Lord, thank You that You can move in the midst of suffering because You've already ultimately moved through it on our behalf.

- What kinds of suffering are you facing today?
- How have you seen suffering produce good things in your life?
- What would it look like if you reminded yourself of the future Jesus secured for you in the face of today's challenges?
- What does the empty tomb say to your current moment of suffering?

Jesus, thank You for taking on all the suffering and sorrow and sin that this world could throw at You, and defeating it all on the cross. Give me strength to remember that when I face suffering, You promise to produce good things in me as I walk through it, for I'm empowered by Your very Spirit and Your empty tomb!

DAY
41

Therefore, if anyone is in Christ, the new creation
has come: The old has gone, the new is here!

2 CORINTHIANS 5:17

I don't know about you, but I get so excited about those moments of the year that offer a new start. Sometimes it's the beginning of a new year. Other times, it's the summer, where families get a fresh experience of spending time together. In other cases, it's the fall, where the school calendar picks back up in August and everyone gets their binders, notebooks, and bookbags, ready to discover what a brand-new school year holds. Sometimes my birthday feels like a fresh start, or simply the changing of the seasons . . . those first warm spring days when the flowers start blooming or those first crisp days of fall.

These moments in our yearly calendar remind me that God always gives us a fresh start, but also that He loves us enough to keep moving us forward from where we once were like we talked about on Day 30 (Phil. 1:6). He's never just repeating the same season over again with nothing to show for it. Instead, He's always moving us onward and upward, transforming us into the image of His Son, even when it doesn't feel like it. He promises that the "old you" has gone—who we once were apart from Christ isn't how God sees us anymore—and that the new creation, the person we were always meant to be, is now here because of Jesus. And more than that, we keep becoming more and more like Him over time. I love that He is continuously making us new, and loving us into the best version of ourselves.

Grateful for the reminder that we are new creations. We aren't the "old" us anymore! No matter how loud lies might be that say otherwise, God's Word speaks a louder Word. If anything or anyone tries to tell us different, let's use these fighting words today: the old has gone, the new has come!

— What times of the year feel like a "new start" for you? Why?

— How did God take you from being an old creation to a new one?

— When do you most often need the reminder that the "old you" is not how God sees you anymore? How might you help yourself remember the truth of this verse in those moments?

🔥 Father, thank You for transforming me from an old creation to a new one! Help me remember that You no longer see who I used to be, but who I am in Christ—and strengthen me to trust that You will never leave me as I am.

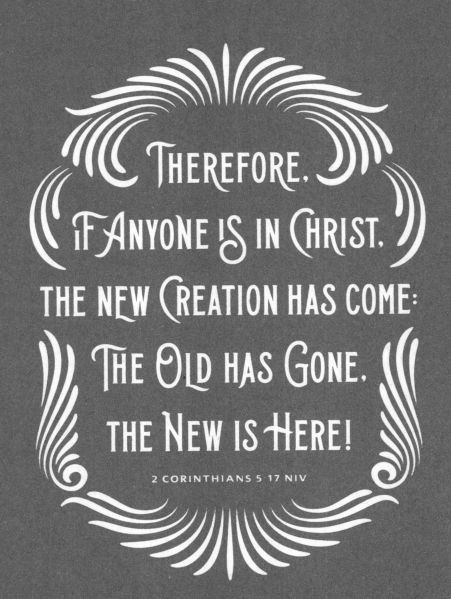

THEREFORE, IF ANYONE IS IN CHRIST, THE NEW CREATION HAS COME: THE OLD HAS GONE, THE NEW IS HERE!

2 CORINTHIANS 5:17 NIV

Guide me in your truth and teach me,
for you are God my Savior,
and my hope is in you all day long.

PSALM 25:5

Have you ever experienced one of those moments where God gives you a certain verse right when you need it? That happened to me recently. In the middle of an intense season of work, I ran across this verse on a calendar, and I was so grateful for the reminder.

Why? Because in addition to a packed schedule, there is also this thing my husband and I are trying to do called parenting, and it is wonderful and rewarding and confounding all in the same breath. There are many moments of clarity and vision that I have as a parent and others when I am at the end of my patience and energy, and I simply don't know how to best shepherd my kids' hearts . . . especially when they are acting like stubborn little sheep!

As I read this verse, God reminded me that He is a good Father and a kind and gentle guide. I often forget (especially on the days when I *myself* am being the stubborn little sheep!) that I can turn from myself and place my hope and trust in *Him*. The days are crazy, but my goodness, when I take just a little time to ask Him for guidance and wisdom, I *never* regret it. He never runs out of energy or patience, and He always finds a way to answer me and lead me— which changes the way I move through the moments of managing whatever chaos I have in front of me.

Maybe you are parenting too. Maybe you're just trying to finish your grocery store run or to-do list. Maybe you're trying to make a big life decision. Wherever you are in this season of life, I'm praying you'll find *hope* in the fact that you don't have to do any of it alone.

- How do you respond when you're in a chaotic season? Are you likely to ask God for guidance, or do you try and do things in your own wisdom and strength?
- Why do you think you sometimes resist asking Him for direction and help?
- How might asking God for guidance change the way you walk through intense or chaotic seasons?
- Write down a memory of a time you asked for God's guidance and He gave it to you. Now write down a memory of when you tried to guide yourself in a stressful situation. Do you notice any differences between the two? What are they?

Lord, help me turn from the hustle of trying to do things in my own strength to the hope of knowing that I can lean into Your guidance. I come to You today and ask You to lead me through whatever crazy or chaos it may bring.

**And my God will meet all your needs according
to the riches of his glory in Christ Jesus.**

PHILIPPIANS 4:19

This promise in God's Word is one I have to keep coming back to over and over in seasons of need. I have faced all kinds of needs, and I'm sure you have too. Sometimes it's related to capacity—I'm all out of energy, and I can't manufacture anymore, yet the day still lies ahead of me, needing me to fully dial in. Other times it's financial, and I've wondered how in the world our family was going to fill the space between what we have and what we need. Still other times it's related to the creativity that's required for songwriting or planning an event or problem-solving. I want to think up new ideas, but I'm all out. Have you been there too?

What I love about this passage in Philippians is that it helps us remember that God is the One who can fill in all those gaps. He meets "all your needs." Not some. *All.* It still floors me to know that His provision for us goes that far—to *all* the places.

I also find solace in this verse because it reminds me of all the times God has provided for people in the Bible, which gives me the hope I need to keep trusting that He'll show up for me in my moments of need. I think of how God provided for Paul through the giving of the church, and how He even provided for Jesus through the giving of some faithful women (Luke 8:3). I think of when Nehemiah needed supplies to rebuild the wall of Jerusalem, and how the Lord gave him all the timber from the forest of a pagan king who didn't even know God—*and* a royal escort from that king's army so Nehemiah would remain safe in the journey (Neh. 2:4–9). I think of Tamar being thirsty in the wilderness, and how God provided a well for her to drink from (Gen. 21:19). I think of how Elijah helped a widow who had little to no food, and how God kept her oil and flour in full supply (1 Kings 17:13–15). I think of Bezalel, who was tasked with making the tabernacle beautiful, and how God provided the creativity and craftsmanship and skill he needed to "make artistic designs" (Exod. 35:30–33). I think of when Joshua needed more time in battle, and how the Lord answered his call and provided more daylight by making the sun stand still (Josh. 10:12–14)! What a wide array of needs, and God provides for them *all*!

Over and over and over again in the Bible, we see the promise of this verse hold true, but when I look back on my own life, I see this promise to be true as well! I can tell story after story of God providing for me personally, for our community, for my kids, for my job, for our church, and my family.

My cousin practices this remembrance of God's provision daily. She writes one or two words to remind her of these kinds of stories on rocks and places them in a bowl in her living room. On days she is struggling to believe the Lord will provide, she goes and picks up a rock that pricks her memory of past provision to give her faith that God will provide again, in one way or another.

I don't know the gaps you need God to fill today in your time, abilities, or resources, but together we can trust that God is able to fill them. Let's rest in that truth today and trust Him for whatever we need, believing that somehow, in ways we might expect (or not expect!), He'll come through for us.

- What is your favorite Bible story of God's provision? Why?

- What needs do you face today? Where are your gaps?

- Are there any areas of your life you assume God can't provide for? How does this verse help free you from that assumption?

— Look back on your life and write down some stories of ways that God has provided for you. Maybe follow my cousin's lead and write these memories down on something you can carry around to jog your memory on the days you're struggling to believe that the Lord is able to meet all your needs.

🔥 Father, You know exactly what my needs are today. I lay it all out before You right now, and trust that in Your own time and in Your own way, You will provide!

Sing and make music from your heart to the
Lord, always giving thanks to God the Father for
everything, in the name of our Lord Jesus Christ.

EPHESIANS 5:19–20

Thankfulness is a practice I often force upon my kids, especially
when they seem disgruntled about something. They sigh a bit, but
they know that I will always respond to whining or complaining by
making them list off things they are grateful for. It can be simple
things. It can be specific or general, but gratitude has a way of bringing beauty and melody into any circumstance or situation (for our
family these days, our list looks like sun, breath, sight, grace, a hot pot
of soup on the stove, any sighting of a dog, and watching our kids fall
in love with *Star Wars*).

I also love that gratitude doesn't negate hardship or pain or even
have to ignore it. In fact, this verse says to give thanks for *everything*.
My mother-in-law talks about this a lot. She says that when she gets
really stressed out, or is in over her head with commitments, or is
facing any kind of conflict or strife, she starts marching around her
house singing out praises to the Lord at the top of her lungs. She'll
thank Him for the struggle, praise Him for His faithfulness, and ask
Him to draw near all in a song that she makes up on the spot! She
also tells me that she always hopes no one walks inside the house
when she's doing it, because they may think she's crazy! I love her.
She talks about how thanking God, even in the midst of difficult situations, genuinely feels like a key to peace and freedom for her. It's
been the same for me.

Thankfulness doesn't always change our circumstances, but so
often when we begin to thank God, even in the midst of really hard or
stressful moments, it invites in a bigger perspective and connects us

to who our Lord really is and all the ways He's blessed us in this life. Cheers to knowing we have a God who is active and present, listening and able. If nothing else, that right there is a reason to sing!

- What would you "sing" to the Lord today and invite Him into? Would it be a song of praise or lament? Try just pouring your heart out before the Lord in the space below. Sing a melody with it if you want to.

- Think about your day today. What about it can you give thanks for? You can be both broad and very specific here.

- Who in your life embodies thankfulness well? Why do you think that's the case?

- Have you ever given God thanks for something difficult in your life? What was that like and what was the result of giving thanks, even in the midst of pain and trouble?

🔥 Father, You tell me to thank You and to make music in my heart in the midst of both ordinary days and challenging ones. Turn my eyes to see the blessings today instead of the things I wish were different.

DAY
45

"You will seek me and find me when you seek me with all
your heart. I will be found by you," declares the LORD.

JEREMIAH 29:13–14A

Have you ever tried to connect to someone else's phone or device using Bluetooth? The process works the same every time. Before you can connect, the owner of the other device has set their phone to be "discoverable." If the other device isn't adjusted to that setting, the connection isn't possible. The other device won't even pop up on your screen—you won't be able to locate it or even know it's there—because it's chosen not to be findable.

A lot of times, we treat God like He's not discoverable, don't we? I know I've done this. I assume He doesn't want to be found by me. Like He's hiding. Or, if He *is* findable to some degree, it requires a whole lot of work and smarts to track Him down. But thankfully, that's not what God says about Himself! I can't get over this reminder in Jeremiah that tells us God is discoverable. He could have stayed fully behind the veil, to the point that we didn't even know He was there. But He didn't. Just look at the language: "I will be found by you." Our God wants to be known and found!

Doesn't that encourage your heart today? The whole reason we can bank on the promise that we'll find God when we seek Him is because He made Himself knowable and discoverable in the first place. If He wanted nothing to do with us, He would have remained off our radar completely. But when we were lost and searching, wondering where He might be, He adjusted the setting to "on." Through creation and His Word and His Son, He has come from behind the veil and revealed Himself. All so that we might deeply know our Maker!

Thank You, Lord for making Yourself knowable to us, for making our connection to You possible. Help us discover more and more of You today and every day!

- Do you sometimes assume God is hiding from you, or doesn't want to be found? Why?
- What truth does this verse and the life and ministry of Jesus speak to those assumptions?
- In what way has God most powerfully revealed Himself to you? Record that memory below.

Father, thank You that while You could have stayed hidden, You made Yourself known! In the moments I am desperately seeking You, help me remember that nothing makes You happier than to be found by me.

For you created my inmost being; you knit me together in
my mother's womb. I praise you because I am fearfully and
wonderfully made; your works are wonderful, I know that
full well. My frame was not hidden from you in the secret
place, when I was woven together in the depths of the earth.
Your eyes saw my unformed body; all the days ordained for
me were written in your book before one of them came to be.
How precious to me are your thoughts, God! How vast is the
sum of them! Were I to count them, they would outnumber
the grains of sand—when I awake, I am still with you.

PSALM 139:13–18

I'll never forget a conversation that I had with my little sister a
few years ago. We were talking about how tiring it is to play the game
of comparison. Comparison makes us feel like we never measure up,
it always steals our joy, and it is usually the beginning of a multitude
of lies that we end up believing about ourselves.

In the middle of the conversation, my sister looked up suddenly
and said this:

> "Well, I don't have time for this anymore. What if
> I actually just took God at His Word and believed
> that what *He* says about me is true?"

What a beautiful and powerful thought! I went home after that
conversation and wrote the song "Wonderfully Made," which still
reminds me of the truth my sister—and God's Word—speak over my
life.

These verses from Psalm 139 have become fighting words for
me. These are the promises I recall when I go to that all-too-familiar

place of self-hatred. When I fall prey to comparison, I try to shift my perspective back to what God says about me. I try to remember that God made us on purpose and for a purpose, and that when He looks at each one of us, He sees us as His precious kids whom He made and loves deeply.

Can you imagine how our lives would look if we *believed* these truths with every fiber of our being instead of *comparing* every fiber of our being with someone else? Every single day, we wake up with the choice on how we will answer my sister's question—What if? What if we actually took God at His Word? What if we deeply and wholly believed that what He says about us is true?

- In what ways or areas of life do you compare yourself with others? In what environments are you most prone to compare?

- How much of your day is spent comparing your life to someone else's? Why do you think you spend this amount of time thinking on such things? Imagine spending that same amount of time thinking on God's Word—how might your life look different if you did this?

- Write out this passage in your own words below. Then, come back to it when you sense the desire to compare rising up.

Father, thank You that You say I am fearfully and wonderfully made! Thank You for the body You gave me, the family You gave me, the life You gave me to live. When I start looking around in comparison, help me to fix my eyes on You instead, and help me believe that what You say about me is true.

While he was in Bethany, reclining at the table in the home
of Simon the Leper, a woman came with an alabaster jar
of very expensive perfume, made of pure nard. She broke
the jar and poured the perfume on his head. Some of those
present were saying indignantly to one another, "Why this
waste of perfume? It could have been sold for more than
a year's wage and the money given to the poor." And they
rebuked her harshly. "Leave her alone," said Jesus. "Why
are you bothering her? She has done a beautiful thing to
me. The poor you will always have with you, and you can
help them any time you want. But you will not always have
me. She did what she could. She poured perfume on my
body beforehand to prepare for my burial. Truly I tell you,
wherever the gospel is preached throughout the world,
what she has done will also be told, in memory of her."

MARK 14:3–9

What a scene here in Mark 14. I'm undone by it every time I read
it. This woman offers Jesus something most precious to her—a jar of
expensive perfume. But the people around her can't see why she'd
do this. When they see the value of the jar, their response is basically,
"What a waste. She could have done way more with what she had."

I don't know about you, but I'm constantly beating myself up for
not doing more with what I have. I have a picture in my head of what
a perfect mom or wife or artist is, one who uses every square inch
of their life in the right ways. But so many days, I don't hit that mark,
and I have to simply offer what I can to Jesus, knowing that in my
broken state, that's the best I can do.

And in that very moment, Jesus meets me with something so kind, just like He did with this woman. "Leave her alone. She's done what she could."

She's done what she could. What words and grace from our mighty Defender. He understands our situation. He knows what we are capable of and what we aren't. And whatever it is that we can give Him, even when we don't get it all the way right, He considers it precious. He knows we've done what we can, He doesn't expect us to be or do more than that, and He defends us against any voice that would say otherwise.

Whatever it is that you're surrendering or offering to God today, and whether or not others might consider it less than what you should have done or even a waste, know that it will be treasured and remembered by Him. Let's rest in that grace that God knows we've done what we could, and He will defend us and love us no matter what.

- In what ways do you beat yourself up?

- Have you ever considered that Jesus is your Defender in those moments? Why or why not?

- How does it make you feel that Jesus knows you've done what you can, and doesn't expect you to do more than that?

Jesus, thank You for being so understanding, and for being my Defender. Help me remember that when I come to You in surrender, what matters is not what other people think of it, but that YOU receive whatever I bring.

DAY
48

Therefore I will boast all the more gladly about
my weaknesses, so that Christ's power may rest
on me. That is why, for Christ's sake, I delight in
weaknesses, in insults, in hardships, in persecutions,
in difficulties. For when I am weak, then I am strong.

2 CORINTHIANS 12:9–10

I have a love/hate relationship with this verse. Why? Truth be told, I don't love feeling weak. I don't like asking for help, and a lot of days, I'm not good at it. Instead, I love feeling capable and strong. But it's this verse that reminds me of a precious truth: it is in my place of being weak and in need that God's love and strength shine.

I learned this recently after dropping the ball with an out-of-town friend when she was walking through a really hard time. Her father had passed very suddenly, and I sent a text about two months afterward to check in on her and to ask if I could send her family a meal. She caught me up via text and said a meal would be lovely. We scheduled the time that I would have it delivered, and y'all . . . I wrote down the wrong day to send her a meal in my calendar and didn't realize it until the day *after* I was supposed to feed her family of seven.

As soon as I realized that I left her stranded without dinner and without even communicating dinner wasn't coming, I text and profusely apologized. She was so gracious and I asked if I could send a meal the next day. We set up the time, and y'all . . . I. FORGOT. AGAIN. Call it that she lives in a different time zone than me. Call it that I have three young kids of my own to feed. Call it that I'm not really a great details person or planner. But honestly, just mainly call me the worst.

I just burst into tears when I realized I'd done it again. I had a pit in my stomach when I made the call and just had to humbly say that I was so sorry. I was trying to relieve stress, and I ended up causing more, and do you know what? She was so gracious again, and instead of just sending her a meal (which I did end up doing the next week, by the way), we actually got to catch up and I got to hear her tell stories about her precious dad and weep with her as she described what it was like to lose him so quickly.

Oh man, as hard as it was to reach out that second time and apologize for being the worst (TWICE in a row), I can remember stopping to confess my weakness and insecurity to God, and asking Him to fill in the gaps for me, to be strong and present in this place I was completely failing in, and wouldn't you know it . . . He turned my blunder into the sweetest conversation that might have never happened if I had simply followed the program and done what I said I was going to do . . . both times. What in the world? Look at the Lord, being strong right in the place where I was weak! Meeting my insufficiency with His more-than-sufficient grace and love. He took what should have made someone want to *quit* being friends with me, and turned it into a grace-covered deep-water connection. It's amazing to watch Him work like that.

Passages like this help me remember that in my moments of imperfection, He is always perfect, and in my moments of being overwhelmed, feeling defeated, in my very weakest places and deepest struggles, His power comes to fight for me. And I can't experience the power if I don't admit I'm weak!

So even though it's counterintuitive, I am learning to not just reluctantly admit when I feel weak, but *rejoice* in those places, and even delight in the moments when I come to the end of myself. Why? Because I'm learning that I'll never come to the end of His strength, and it's usually the moments when I'm at the end of my rope that I encounter His love and mercy in the most powerful ways. (I'd also like to add that I did learn how to set alerts on my calendar, which has been a *very* helpful feature to help support my lack of logistical prowess! Thank You, Lord!!)

- How do you usually respond when you are feeling weak or insecure?

- What usually holds you back from inviting Christ into your weakness?

- Have you ever "boasted" in your weaknesses? What if we tried that together here? Write down one place of weakness, insecurity, or hardship in your life, and then follow it up by recording the ways that God shows Himself strong in those places.

🔥 Lord, I have spent much of my life hiding my weakness because I believed the lie that I am supposed to be "good" or "perfect" all on my own. Thank You that while none of us can be good enough to reach perfection, Jesus was good enough. He was perfect for us, so His perfect life could be a covering for ours. Help me to turn from my weakness to Your strength, so I don't miss out on the power of the gospel—a power that reaches into my deepest moments of failure and applies grace and mercy there.

Oh give thanks to the LORD . . . for his love endures
forever! Let the redeemed of the LORD say so.

PSALM 107:1–2A ESV

As I've mentioned before, one of my favorite things that I've had
the privilege of doing is serving at Young Life camps over the years.
By way of reminder, Young Life is a para-church organization that
believes every kid everywhere deserves to hear the gospel in a way
that they can comprehend and understand. Volunteer Young Life
leaders build relationships with students throughout the year and
bring kids to camps each summer to hear the story of the gospel.
At the end of a week at camp, there is a gathering called a "Say So,"
inspired by this verse. It's a meeting where they pass around a micro-
phone in a room full of hundreds of kids, and those who decided to
begin a relationship with Christ stand up and "say so." Being in that
room full of kids, each with their own story to tell of how God's love
has rescued them, is a powerful thing.

I don't know about you, but I want to be like those kids. I want
to tell the stories of how God has moved in my life, and thank Him.
I want to "say so" when I see His hand at work, blessing me with
His great help, kindness, and love. Why? Because my heart starts to
move into a hopeful place when I stop to count the gifts in my life
and express thanks for each one. My soul is always strengthened
as I tell the stories in my life that bear witness to God's faithfulness.
Somehow, through giving Him thanks and praise and remembering
His work in my life, I move from grumbling to gracious. And I have a
sneaking suspicion that He made the process of giving thanks that
way on purpose—as if God knows it's good for us. I think He knows,
too, that because of His enduring love, we will always have a story
to tell.

I pray today that the Lord would help us hold tightly to His goodness and enduring love, and I pray He'll give us the strength to practice thankfulness and enjoy the way that it turns our hearts from complaining and comparison to praise and storytelling. Lord, continue to help us "say so" when we've seen Your hand move in our lives. Help us practice telling our redemption stories and giving thanks, always.

- What stories can you tell of God's faithfulness and goodness to you? List some in the space provided below.

- When was the last stretch of your life that you can look back on and say, "Wow, I was really consumed with thankfulness in that season"? What do you think caused such thankfulness? Or, if you cannot think of a season like that, why do you think this is the case?

- How could you instill a regular practice of "saying so" in your life?

- How might instilling a regular practice of "say so" / "telling God-stories" change the way you see God working and showing up in your daily life?

Lord, help me notice the ways Your hand has moved—and is moving!—in my life, and once I do, help me say so. Give me the strength to continue telling redemption stories and the power to stay in a place of gratitude and praise.

DAY
50

You turned my wailing into dancing; you removed
my sackcloth and clothed me with joy, that my
heart may sing to you and not be silent. O LORD
my God, I will give you thanks forever.

PSALM 30:11-12

This verse has woven its way into several of my songs ("Broken Beautiful" and "Love Broke Through"). Why? Because I've seen God do this in my life over and over again, and I can't get over it. We talked about redemption stories yesterday, and how powerful they are. When I look back and think about the specifics of those stories, I realize that they are not stories of how faithful and holy I've been, but about how faithful *God* has been to meet me in my worst moments. It's backward and upside-down, but I can trace His goodness and mercy back to every single time my heart has been heavy or broken or full of shame. He has shown up to offer His love to me over and over again.

If you're in a season of wailing, know that you are not alone . . . and that this moment is not the way your story will ultimately end. We are free to lament the evil and brokenness in this world, but we also have good reason to look forward to the hope Christ offers us. He took on death, and He defeated it. And there is coming a day when He will finish it off for good. This means you and I can mourn and lament and wail in the moments we need to, but we can also take heart in those very same moments, knowing God and only God has the ability to turn that agony around into joy one day. That's the kind of God He is. He can't help but make broken things beautiful. We can hold onto this truth about our God, no matter why we might be wailing today. Not because it's a nice thing to think about, but because it really is *true*.

Your love will never change, there's healing in Your name
You can take broken things and make them beautiful
You took my shame and You walked out of the grave
So Your love can take broken things and make them beautiful

//

You say that You'll turn my weeping into dancing
Remove my sadness and cover me with joy
You say Your scars are the evidence of healing
That You can make the broken beautiful
—The Broken Beautiful

- Why is it sometimes hard to hold both pain and hope together in tension?

- What evil or broken things in our world might you need to take some time and lament today?

- Where might you need to fight to hold on to the future hope Christ promises you more than you have been?

Father, thank You for showing up in places where I once "wailed," or am now wailing, with hope and joy in Your hands. Please make beautiful things out of my brokenness today, and help me trust You will one day defeat all broken things in full.

"The thief comes only to steal and kill and destroy; I have come that they may have life, and have it to the full."

JOHN 10:10

You know those Bible verses that you just adore? The ones that always seem to speak life over you, no matter the situation? The ones that you just keep coming back to? This is one of those for me. I love this verse. I have always loved it.

When I was much younger, I used to think that this verse was simply a promise for a wonderful life *full* of good things, and while I have certainly experienced a wonderful life full of so many gifts from God, I don't think that is what Jesus means here. I think it means so much more.

As I have walked through a good deal of sorrow and loss, what I have encountered even in those hard, dark places, is the abundance of God's love and comfort and mercy. While a life full of tangible blessings is so wonderful to experience at times, they can't get you through the darkness in the way God's presence and character can. In the bountiful places and the empty ones, *He's* the real blessing we crave. *He's* the true gift we seek. *He's* the vibrant life we desire. No matter who or what tries to steal it away from us, He's where the abundance is.

I can't tell you how many times I have been in the middle of a shame storm (those moments when the lies are loud, my mistakes are the only thing that I can see, and it feels like the shadows are closing in whispering that not only did I do something wrong, but that *I am* wrong), and this verse will come to mind. In the midst of a deluge of lies that I'm being pelted by, one of the biggest being that I am all alone, this verse reminds that there is a thief who wants to steal every shred of joy, confidence, dignity, gratitude, and health in me. It's one of those verses that feels like a bucket of cold water on your face, and when I'm able to remember it, it wakes me up and jolts me into the truth. It reminds me that there's nothing new under the sun. The thief still hates it when I am secure and confident and free and *alive* knowing that I belong and I'm beloved, *but* Jesus always stands steadily, full of abundant life and ready to flush out all the lies with all His love.

So thankful today that God comes to give us life to the full—the abundance of Himself in the full scope of all we experience in this life. So thankful we have a vibrancy that we can tap into whether we are in the heights of our joy or the depths of our sorrow. Lord, may You bring this verse to mind in the moments we need it the most.

- In what ways have you experienced the effects of the enemy, who comes to steal, kill, and destroy?

- To where, whom, or what do you typically run to find "abundance" or "life"?

- How is God a better source of abundant life than that thing or person?

Lord, help me remember to lean into the fullness of all that You are in both moments of gladness and grief. Help me see and believe that You are where vibrant life is found, and when I stray to find life somewhere else, help me return to You.

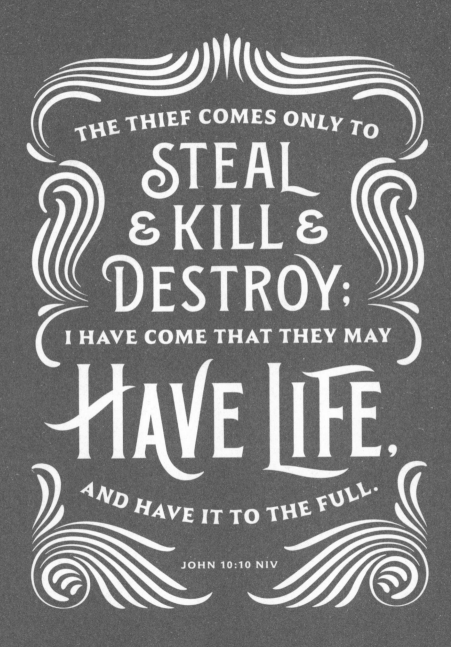

THE THIEF COMES ONLY TO
STEAL
& KILL &
DESTROY;
I HAVE COME THAT THEY MAY
HAVE LIFE,
AND HAVE IT TO THE FULL.

JOHN 10:10 NIV

But I trust in you, LORD; I say, "You are my God." My
times are in your hands; deliver me from the hands
of my enemies, from those who pursue me.

PSALM 31:14–15

Have you ever been in a season that feels hard and unbearable? Have you ever felt pursued by some sort of enemy? Have you ever wondered "How long, oh Lord?" Have you ever looked around at your circumstances and wondered if they were actually in good hands?

I've been there too, and I cannot tell you the number of times I have had to remind my soul that, "My times are in Your hands." David wrote this psalm from a desperate and overwhelming place, surrounded by enemies, and in the midst of all of this, he reminds his weary soul that his trust isn't in his circumstances, his trust is in the Lord.

Oh may we remember, especially when the suffering feels so long, the road feels so hard, and the enemies seem so strong, that our times are in His hands, and that He is a good God who can help us, and hears our prayers for deliverance. It does our souls such good to remember that our hope is not in our circumstances, but in a good and faithful God who will not ever change no matter the circumstance. May we fight to remember like David did that He's got us, even in the desperate and overwhelming places.

Our lives, our circumstances—our *everything*—are in His hands. And those hands are trustworthy hands. May we remember that together right now as we brave whatever today holds.

- Where in your life does it feel you are facing something unbearable, or perhaps like an enemy is pursuing you? In this situation, what or whom do you typically trust for deliverance? Why?

- How does Jesus' example help you place your life in the hands of God even when the situation is painful and bleak (Luke 23:46)?

- How do you know the Lord's hands are good hands, worthy enough to hold your everything? What have His hands done for you (Luke 24:36–40)?

🔥 Father, help me to place my times in Your hands like David and Jesus did. Give me the strength to trust in You instead of my circumstances, even when the road feels hard, and help me remember You are a good and faithful God who will never change in Your love for me.

DAY
53

By day the LORD directs his love, at night his song
is with me—a prayer to the God of my life.

PSALM 42:8

I cannot tell you how much this verse means to me. It is a promise that has carried me through a few seasons of suffering. It's the verse that inspired a song I wrote called "Night Song." I kept wondering, "If God's song is with me at night, what are the words? How does that chorus go?"

I sing to my kids almost every night that I put them to bed, and it's usually my favorite part of the day. No matter how crazy the day has been, no matter how many times they haven't listened and gotten themselves into trouble, no matter how many tears there were, we end the day the same way: I read to them and hold them and kiss them and remind them of who they are and how I love them, and I sing.

And this sort of thing isn't just something my kids need at the end of a long, hard day. It's something I need too. This verse reminds *me* that before I am a mom, before I'm an adult with a lot of different responsibilities, I am first and foremost a beloved daughter of God. I'm His kid, and no matter how crazy my day has been and no matter how many mistakes and messes I make, at the end of the day, He still loves me and holds me and reminds me of who I am. "At night, his song is with me."

Whatever kind of day you're having, I hope today's verse reminds you that you are still loved and held and cared for by your heavenly Father. God, may we take a deep breath, and rest in Your love that is with us both day *and* night. May we lean into Your arms and find the joy of knowing You sing over us, no matter how crazy the day has been.

- What things do you run to for comfort at the end of a long day?

- What about today—or this week—tempts you to believe God won't meet you with kindness, comfort, and help at the end of it?

- Remembering that you are God's child, how can you help yourself experience the truth that "at night his song is with you"? According to Zephaniah 3:17, Isaiah 62:5, and Psalm 139, what do God's songs over you say?

Father, thank You for being a heavenly parent who wraps me up in the truth at the end of every day. Help me remember You're with me, day and night, no matter what life brings, and help me to listen more intently to the night songs You sing over me.

Rejoice always, pray continually, give thanks in all
circumstances; for this is God's will for you in Christ Jesus.

1 THESSALONIANS 5:16–18

This verse is such a sweet reminder for me. How often do I forget to pray? *A lot.* I worry about things. I try to control things. I talk to friends and ask for people's advice. I say that I "need to pray about this," but so often, I wait so long to get down to the business of praying. And yet right here is God's command to "pray continually."

One of my sweet friends tells me that when there is a lot on her mind, she just talks it out with God. She speaks it all out in His direction. What a beautiful way of looking at prayer. Whenever I begin to direct my joy, my desires, my doubt, my cries for help, my worry toward Jesus, something changes in my heart. And I have a sneaking suspicion on why that happens—because I'm living right in the middle of God's will for me! Did you catch that part about this passage? We don't have to fret about finding what God's will is for our life—it's right here! When we rejoice, pray, and give thanks, there's no question or doubt: we're living in God's will.

Isn't that amazing? Doesn't it take the burden off? Today, even in the midst of being tired and feeling like we don't have enough energy, skill, and endurance to pull off all that we need to, we can rejoice in knowing that as long as we are praying it all out in God's direction, we're still in the center of His will for our lives. We haven't gone off track! God's will isn't held hostage from us, in some secret place only accessible to the super spiritual or smart, but instead is simply in the daily practice of talking continually with our God. How freeing is that?!

- What usually holds you back from continual prayer? Rejoicing always? Giving thanks in all circumstances?

- How has this passage helped free you up when it comes to the idea of God's will for your life?

- What are some things you need to rejoice and give thanks for? List them below and speak them out in His direction.

Lord, thank You for commands like this, given not because You are out to restrict me, but because Your heart is for my good and for me to draw near to You. Help me to remember that as long as I'm praying continually, rejoicing, and giving thanks, I'm right at the center of Your will for me!

"But while he was still a long way off, his father saw him and was filled with compassion for him; he ran to his son, threw his arms around him and kissed him."

LUKE 15:20

Do you have any favorite stories in Scripture? I have many, but one that has been jumping out at me lately is the story of the prodigal son. This is my favorite part. I love it so much. It's not just that the father has compassion for his son—it's that he must have been looking every day at the horizon, waiting and hoping for the day his boy might come home, and the *moment* the father catches a glimpse of his son, he *runs* to embrace him. He was ready and waiting, feet postured to hit the pavement when his beloved child was barely in view.

This is striking enough for us when we read it, but it was even more unbelievable for the people who originally heard this story as Jesus told it. In that day and time, fathers didn't run at all. They didn't pick up their robe to move quickly. To do so would be totally undignified, especially for a wayward son who seriously screwed up and offended the family. But Jesus says this father is what God is like! Undignified in His love for us, even when we screw up!

When I screw up, my tendency is to hide. Is that true for you too? I think that comes from a misunderstanding of God's love for me. His love isn't based on how well we're doing or on how much we have screwed up. God's not out to get us. He's out to draw us near. He's out to hit the ground running toward us in love.

Lord, help me remember, especially when I fall on my face and make mistakes, that You are full of compassion for us, that You've got your eyes on the horizon, ready to run to us and wrap us in Your arms. Grateful for mercy today and for the embrace of a Father who is surprisingly undignified in His love for us.

- Think of a moment you felt deep compassion for someone else. Describe what that was like.

- When you miss the mark in some way, how do you picture God's face toward you? What sort of expression is He making? What sort of posture is He taking?

- How does this passage square with the picture of God you just envisioned?

Lord, I can sense the pull to run away from You in fear, especially when I make mistakes—help me fight that tendency, and instead, run headlong into Your compassionate arms. Thank You for being a Father who is undignified and extravagant in His love for me, ready to receive me in any moment I come running!

"Blessed are those who mourn,
for they will be comforted."

MATTHEW 5:4

There is much to grieve in our own lives, in our country, and in our world today, and this verse gives me so much hope. It reminds me that when I am in a place of great grief or sorrow, I am not the only one. There is comfort for the taking. Somehow in the economy of the gospel, those who mourn will still be blessed, because there is a promise of comfort. I don't ever wish sorrow or grief on anyone, including myself, but my goodness, I am so grateful to have known the sweet comfort of the presence of God when my heart has been broken. I can tell story after story of this in my life.

Here's one of them:

My birthday is September 12th, and in the wake of all the tragedy that struck September 11, 2001, I woke up on my birthday with a heart as heavy as stone. As an eighteen-year-old, newly in college and out in the world on my own for the first time, the chaos of what happened to the Twin Towers and the Pentagon felt so deeply confusing. I was so sad. I was scared. I missed home. I wanted to be with my family.

My mom and dad called to wish me a happy birthday, and I sounded depressed over the phone. They consoled me, listened, and then encouraged me to get out of bed and open up my curtains to let some light in the room. When I did, I *fell* out of my bed that was right by the window! Standing outside my dorm room window were my mom and dad with balloons and bagels. I wept. I needed comfort, and they drove three hours to give it to me at just the right moment.

For those who are grieving today, I'm so sorry. I'm lifting you up today and asking the Lord to bring you the comfort you need. Know today that He is near, and He blesses those in mourning. He is faithful to come and console. Let's run into His arms today, trusting Him for that blessing.

- What are you mourning over these days?
- If you are not lamenting over something today, is there anything in your past you might need to mourn with the Lord? Anything that you've haven't quite processed or made the time for?
- If you are not in a season of mourning, how might God be asking you to show up and be a presence of love and comfort for someone else who is?

Lord, thank You for being a God that comforts us when we mourn. Give me the courage to trust You today with my sorrows. You know what they are—help me to collapse into Your arms, and give me a sense of Your comfort even now.

... And he gave us this wonderful message of
reconciliation. So we are Christ's ambassadors;
God is making his appeal through us.

2 CORINTHIANS 5:19B–20 NLT

If you have children, you know that they have their super sweet moments. The ones that make your heart want to explode because you can't handle the cuteness. But, at the same time, you also know they have those moments that we'd call anything but sweet. They fight and quarrel and tattletale. One steals the other's toy. The other throws a fit because their toy was stolen. One breaks a rule and the others make sure Mom or Dad know about it immediately. In their anger toward each other, the work of parenthood is teaching them what *reconciling* looks like. It's the work of being brought together when they were once at odds, of making peace where there was once nothing but hostility.

Reconciliation is a beautiful thing, and it's not just a random part of parenting for me. It's actually one of my favorite upside-down parts of the gospel itself. We are broken and sinful, *but God* sent His Son, bringing *both* justice and freedom, on the cross where Jesus gave up His life for ours. We get His righteousness for our brokenness, and the result? We get to be reconciled to a God we were once at odds with. We get to be at peace with a Father we once were separated from. All because of Christ. And if that weren't enough, you know what floors me? After all that reconciling work Jesus did between us and the Father, God then calls us not only to sit and enjoy it, but He also calls us onward, to carry the gospel message of reconciliation wherever we go.

What does that mean? It means that where there is brokenness, fighting, and hostility, we show up with love and humility to be reconciled and made whole as far as it is up to us. What a beautiful way to live. Having had the privilege of seeing this fleshed out in so many relationships, I'm not sure there is any work that is more beautiful. It is *hard*, but it is good. So Lord, help me be about this work of reconciliation wherever I go and for all of my days; both online and in person, may I be someone who sows seeds of reconciliation rather than division and hostility. Thank You that you brought the message first, through Jesus, and that because of Him, we can move forward with faithfulness to seek reconciliation wherever we are and in whatever we do.

— How does it feel to know that Jesus made it possible for you to be forever reconciled with God?

— When you look outside at the world, where do you see obvious examples of hostility, brokenness, and fighting? Where do you see the same things in your own life and relationships?

— What would doing the work of reconciliation look like in those spaces? How might God be calling you to be an ambassador of peace this week?

Jesus, thank You for reconciling me to God! Please teach me to follow after You in being a person of reconciliation wherever I go, and embolden me to be an ambassador of Your message and Your peace even in the midst of disagreement and division.

DAY
58

"Simply let your 'Yes' be 'Yes,' and your 'No' be 'No.'"

MATTHEW 5:37

When it comes to giving our word about something (or our time), Jesus is so kind to give us such a simple principle to follow. No seven-point plan. No intense sermon. Simply "let your yes be yes" and "let your no be no." It's like Jesus is telling us, "When you say yes to something, don't halfway show up for it. Really show up for it. When you say *no*, don't backtrack or reconsider a million times or make apologies. Be okay with the fact that you needed to say no. Whatever your answer, keep your word and mean what you say. Decide which answer is wisest in each case, and then be at rest with your decision."

You'd think that because this principle is simple, it would be easy. But for me? It's not. I read this verse recently and was so convicted. There is such wisdom here that I do not employ day to day in my life. Namely, I say "yes" to way too much. I'm a 7 on the Enneagram and I want to do everything. (If you don't know what that is, it means I'm interested in all the things and that I don't want to miss out on anything, so I often end up doing way too much all at once!)

Have you ever felt that way? Like you don't want "either/or"? Like you don't want to have to choose? I can relate so deeply. I want "both/and" almost all the time, so I agree to much more than I can actually pull off, and it inevitably causes problems with my schedule. And if it not my schedule, it causes problems with my focus. I sometimes have trouble fully showing up to the task at hand because I'm distracted by the tons of other things on my mind (or I'm coming out of the last thing I said yes to, and all my energy is drained). I had good intentions when I took on something new, but I couldn't show up and *mean* it the way I wanted to. I said yes, but halfway. I didn't keep my word—not fully. I let my default answer get in the way of the wise one.

I am grateful today that Jesus not only gives us the principle; He also shows us the way. His life is full of times He wisely said "yes" or "no," and as we read His Word, we can learn from Him on how to create good boundaries in our lives. And on top of showing us His example, He also has the power to help us when we stumble and fall. I pray for myself and for you today, that we'd follow His beautiful example, and that when we forget—or in the moments we mean well but get it wrong—we'd run into the arms of our Savior who can dust us off, wrap us up in love, and help us take the next wise step.

- Do you lean more toward saying "yes" too much? Or do you lean more toward saying "no"? Why do you think this is your default answer?

- Since I strongly dislike saying "no," my counselor always tells me that when I have to say "no" to something, it helps to picture what that "no" is allowing me to say "yes" to. What might you need to say "no" to right now?

- Would you say you're a person who keeps your word? How does managing your time well and drawing good boundaries relate to keeping your word?

Lord, help me to be wise with my words and my time. Teach me to draw good boundaries, and help me to learn that saying "No" to "more" can often be the most loving thing that I can do.

Even though I walk through the valley of the shadow
of death, I will fear no evil, for you are with me;
your rod and your staff, they comfort me.

PSALM 23:4

"Even though . . ." What a beautiful beginning to a prayer.

Even though I'm facing another uncertain season of work.

Even though I'm braving another tough issue in marriage.

Even though I'm changing yet another diaper.

Even though I'm running into the same relational difficulty with a loved one.

Even though I'm still not entering in that phase of life I desperately want to enjoy.

Even though I'm looking again at an empty bank account.

Even though I'm wrestling with that same health issue that won't seem to let up.

Even though I'm still laying down my dreams for someone else's.

Even though I'm met by another valley in a journey that's already been so difficult.

I don't know what it is for you. But as you begin today with "Even though . . ."—fill in the blank with whatever hardship or loss you are facing today—you can resolutely follow that up with, "I will fear no evil, for You are *with* me."

I'm so thankful for God's kind company today no matter what we face. This verse has served me well to fight back fear in the face of the many valleys I have passed through. I hope it serves you too.

I hope it helps you fight to believe that being with God in the valley is better than being without Him on the mountaintop. This verse gives me fresh faith to remember that because of God's presence, we don't have to fear the "even thoughs" in our lives right now, no matter what they are.

Lies say the valley is too deep for God to reach you. But God says He's there, keeping you company no matter how long it lasts. Lord, help us stand in the power of this truth today.

- What is your version of "even though"?

- Recall a time that you were on a "mountaintop" in the world's eyes, but far from God's presence. What was that experience like?

- Why do you think you often believe the lie that the valley is too deep for God to reach you? How might you better fight this lie in the future?

Father, thank You for Your kindness to me in the valley. Help me remember that I'm not alone in it—that You are with me. Give me the strength to fight the lie that this valley is mine to brave by myself, and renew my trust in Your presence.

If you'd like to sing this psalm with me, it's written into the song called "All of My Days" on my album, *All of My Days.*

Cast all your anxiety on him because he cares for you.

1 PETER 5:7

Do you ever feel like you are *constantly* carrying things? For me, a lot of days I have a purse on my shoulder, a child on my hip, keys looped on my finger, a phone in my back pocket, a coffee mug in my hand, work gear crammed into my backpack, grocery bags from the store weighing down my elbow—and sometimes all of these things at once! Do you ever feel like there are days when you're literally holding it all together, like your hands never see a moment when they aren't totally full?

Lately I've been noticing the things I carry. And sometimes, I don't have the option of casting certain things off of myself. But you know what? Sometimes I *do*. Some things were never meant for me to carry. For example, how many days do I walk around carrying worry, fears, and anxiety? *So* many. I'll carry my own, and also anxieties of other people I love. While God's Word does tell us to bear each other's burdens, I forget that we can only do that with God's help. Instead of leaning into that help, I often hold all of these things at once, feeling like it's all on me to help make it all better.

The word *cast* means to "throw something forcefully in a specified direction." When it comes to the things we aren't supposed to carry, I am praying today that we will *throw* everything that worries us in the direction of the One who cares for us best. He can handle it much better than we can, and we weren't made to carry it alone anyway.

Lord, help us walk forward today holding onto the things You have called us to carry, throwing off the things You haven't, and believing that our anxieties are better placed in Your caring hands than in our own.

- What anxieties are you carrying around today?

- Why do you sometimes keep certain burdens on your own shoulders instead of transferring them over onto the shoulders of God?

- God's Word not only tells us what we aren't meant to carry, but also the things we *are* meant to carry! For example, we are called to "carry this precious Message [of the gospel] around in . . . our ordinary lives" (2 Cor. 4:7 MSG). Similarly, we are also called to "carry the light-giving Message into the night" (Phil. 2:14–16 MSG). How might you take some time today to trade the things you *aren't* made to carry for the things you are made to carry?

God, You know the anxieties I've been carrying all by myself. Help me to throw my worries forcefully in Your direction and help me carry instead the bright light of Your life-giving love!

"A new command I give you: Love one another. As I have
loved you, so you must love one another. By this everyone
will know that you are my disciples, if you love one another."

JOHN 13:34–35

Do you ever wonder what it would've been like to be one of Jesus' disciples during His earthly ministry? I'm sure there were lots of moments the disciples had to face the strife and division all around them, as well as the weariness within them. Yet there also must have been lots of moments of joy and brotherhood and adventure. It's easier for me to imagine what it must have been like to do life alongside Jesus. What's harder is imagining how it felt for them to face His departure after years at the side of the Jesus, learning and laughing and laboring.

What would that have been like? The man who marked them as a group wouldn't walk among them anymore. How would they maintain their identity as His followers once He was gone? Sure, the world could certainly identify them as Jesus-followers when Jesus Himself was leading the pack, in the flesh for all to see. But once He was gone from plain view, how would the world know who the "Jesus people" were? What would mark them?

John 13 gives us a glimpse. Jesus is telling His disciples that He will only be with them a little longer, and He leaves them with this beautiful command: Love one another. Of everything He could have said, He said that. Love. But not just any love. Love "as I have loved you." There are so many days that I tend to overcomplicate things. Our culture feels very divided and angry right now, as I'm sure it felt for the disciples at times, and this verse helps me ask myself this question in every scenario: "How can I love here? Even if we disagree

. . . even if we look at the world so differently? How can I love as I have been loved?"

I don't know how to love well in certain places of tension especially, but I think it might start with more listening and kindness as Christians. After all, the world has to look somewhere to see what love is like. Shouldn't it be best displayed in Jesus' people? I love that Jesus didn't say, "Convince everyone that I am real! Beat it over their heads." He said, "Love one another." The way He loves us. That's the word Jesus spoke over His disciples before He left. That's His plan for how the world might know how real He truly is. That's what should mark us in this world. You and me and all our brothers and sisters in the family of God loving each other, and loving our neighbors too; this is the way people identify where the presence of Christ is! Oh, that we would listen and embody this call from the Lord to love as He has loved us.

- Why do you think Christians fail to love each other sometimes?

- Who might you need to reconcile with, in order to rightly reflect the love Jesus calls us to embody in this passage?

- How would you describe the way that God has loved you personally? In what ways could you ask God to expand your heart to embody His love more fully?

Lord, would You help me to be a person marked by Your love, and would You teach me how to love more like You love all of us?

A NEW COMMAND I GIVE YOU:

LOVE ONE ANOTHER.

 AS I HAVE LOVED YOU, SO
YOU MUST LOVE ONE ANOTHER.

BY THIS EVERYONE WILL KNOW

THAT YOU ARE MY DISCIPLES,

IF YOU LOVE ONE ANOTHER.

JOHN 13 34–35 NIV

DAY
62

On God rests my salvation and my glory;
my mighty rock, my refuge is God.

PSALM 62:7 ESV

When the winds of life or stress or change blow hard, where do you run to feel safe? When the waters rise or the storm rolls in, where do you seek shelter?

As I look back on my life, I can see lots of flimsy shelters that I tried to run to, hoping for security and strength and safety in the midst of the storm. One of them is control over my circumstances. *If I can just find a way to make this work out, I'll be safe.* Another one is what other people think of me. *If I can just come off the right way in this situation, it'll all be okay.* Other times, the refuge hasn't been so metaphorical. It's been my actual house! *If I can just get into that one place that feels like a better fit for my family—and finally getting it running smoothly and looking a certain way—we'll all be able to breathe a bit better.*

Maybe all that sounds familiar to you. Or maybe the place of refuge for you looks different, but you can resonate with the temptation to find all your security in something that eventually breaks down on you. No matter what shape our temporary refuges take, over and over we learn the same lesson: it wasn't as strong as we thought it would be. Because it isn't God. It isn't our Savior. It's never going to be what Jesus can be for us when the winds come blowing and the water starts to rise.

This verse reminds me of the song we used to sing in Sunday school. "The foolish man built his house upon the sand." In that song, after the rains come down and floods come up, what happens to that house on the sand? It falls down, but the house built on the rock? It stood firm! I remember taking my little fist and hammering down on my other hand when we sang that particular line. "And the house on the rock stood firm!" I'm so grateful that when the storms of life come our way, we have a firm foundation on the mighty rock of Jesus. I'm so thankful for the refuge that Jesus is for us, a place where we can find our identity, our security, and endless supply of love and faithfulness. May we take heart in this and find our refuge and rest in God, who loves us deeply.

- What temporary refuge are you most tempted to run into when the winds of life blow hard?
- How has that source of security failed you in the past?
- How has God proven Himself a better refuge than all others in your life?

Oh Lord, help me to remember today that YOU are my rock and my refuge . . . not my circumstances, not my reputation, not my family or my home or my job. You are my safest place to run. Help me run into You today, no matter what I face.

"The LORD will fight for you;
you need only to be still."

EXODUS 14:14

You've heard me mention that my husband, Drew, and I walked through an immense season—about four years long—of impossibly hard situations. We felt like the waters were constantly rising, like there was no way through. This Exodus verse comes from one of the stories in God's Word that was extremely hope-inducing to me during that season.

After years of being enslaved, Moses finally comes to set the Israelites free. They are running away and suddenly find themselves in an impossible situation. They come to the Red Sea, have no way of crossing it, and there is an army in pursuit of them. They basically panic and say to Moses in this moment, "Did you free us from slavery so you could bury us in the desert?" I love their honesty because that is how it feels some days, doesn't it? Some days I find myself praying, "God, I know You are good, but *this* situation that I'm in the middle of? It's *not* good. It's breaking my heart." And there in the midst of all of that fear and doubt, Moses speaks these words over the panicked Israelites: "The LORD will fight for you."

If you're familiar with the story, you know what happens. God opens up the Red Sea, and the Israelites walk on the ocean floor! And you know what? They didn't go by themselves; God was trailing them from behind, standing in between them and their enemies! This is what I saw God do for me and for our people as we walked through seasons of panic and confusion and "impossible"—seasons that we were sure would swallow us whole. We encountered Jesus there, standing with us like God did with the Israelites, and He reminded us that we don't have to bury our hope because Hope *Himself* was already buried for us, and He walked up out of the grave!

This is the verse and the story that my song "Red Sea Road" is anchored into, and I wrote it to remind myself that even in the midst of our desert places, in the midst of impossibly sorrowful seasons, God shows up and makes a way for us to carry on when it feels like we can't carry on any longer.

Are you panicked? Are you confused today, wondering if there's a way out of the place you are in? You need only to be still. The Lord your God will fight for you and He will lead you through.

> *We will sing to our souls, We won't bury our hope*
> *Where He leads us to go, there's a Red Sea Road*
> *When we can't see the way, He will part the waves*
> *And we'll never walk alone down a Red Sea Road*

- What impossible situations do you find yourself in the middle of right now?

- What lies are you tempted to believe about yourself or God when you are feeling panicked like this? What are the honest cries of your heart?

- What steps could you take to "be still" and rest in the power and love of God for you today?

God, You know what "impossible" means for me today. Help me to be still in the midst of it, and give me the strength to turn to You and remember that You will fight for me. You will carry me when I don't have the strength to carry on, and You are a God who makes a way out of no way!

The LORD will be your everlasting light.

ISAIAH 60:20B

What's your favorite season of the year? I love spring for so many reasons. The whole earth is telling the story that death isn't the end. Things may look bleak and winter may feel long. Maybe it's a stretch of time where a deep desire is not fulfilled. Maybe it's a relationship that simply won't mend, though you've tried and tried to patch things up. Maybe it's a physical or spiritual battle you've fought for years, only to wake up having to fight again. Maybe it's a season of financial strain or painful betrayal. Whatever it looks like for you, winter seasons come for us all at some point. Cold. Dark. And seemingly endless.

But spring always comes at some point, singing a defiant song: life is coming. Hope is coming. When I see flowers start to shoot up out of the ground and little bright green buds of leaves on the end of brown branches, I am reminded we have good reason to hope, because the Lord will be our everlasting light.

May we remember this when we are in seasons that feel like a *long*, dark winter. In the places that feel so bleak, let us remind our weary hearts that spring is coming and that God's light *will* shine down on us and make the coldness melt away. May we remember that because of the gospel work of Jesus—because our sins were nailed to His cross and because the grave couldn't hold Him down—winter will not last forever! The Lord will be our everlasting light.

- What season of the year most reminds you of God's promises and care?

- What would a picture of "spring" look like for you right now, if all your plans worked out?

- If that picture doesn't pan out for you in the end, what sort of "spring" does God say you can definitely bank on? What picture is definitely coming?

Thank You, Lord, for being my everlasting light. Help me believe spring is coming on my cold and dark days, and give me new life in Your light.

Therefore each of you must put off falsehood and speak truthfully to your neighbor, for we are all members of one body. "In your anger do not sin." Do not let the sun go down while you are still angry, and do not give the devil a foothold.

EPHESIANS 4:25–27

I know that one of the tactics of the enemy to steal, kill, and destroy is to keep us believing lies, but I can so easily forget that he's got another tactic up his sleeve, and that's keeping us in anger.

Do you notice anything in particular that flares anger up in your heart? For me it can be anything from traffic jams, to miscommunications, to feeling misunderstood or unfairly criticized on social media. While it's not always wrong to be angry (sometimes we have righteous reasons for feeling that way), we are told two things in this passage: 1) to not sin in that anger, and 2) to not let the sun go down while we are still angry. In other words, we shouldn't stay angry long. If we let it linger, taking up residence in our hearts and extending its roots deep into our souls, we "give the devil a foothold." Heaven knows I don't want him getting any kind of foothold in my life, much less a millimeter!

Dealing with anger in my heart before it has the time to drive roots down into my heart has taken *a lot* of work of "speaking truthfully to my neighbor." It's not easy. It's required so many hard marital conversations before bed, when all I want to do is ignore the problem and just go to bed. It's required me to stop and deal with the tantrums of my kids when I'd rather just go on my porch and fume. It's required me to pick up the phone and sort out a miscommunication with a friend when it feels super uncomfortable to do so. But you know what? I never regret it. Usually, if I take the time to acknowledge the anger in the moment instead of letting it boil over, seeking to solve whatever problem is behind it and speak truthfully about how I'm feeling, the anger doesn't linger nearly as long, and sometimes it even evaporates! Unconfronted and unworked-through anger often drives a wedge into relationships, but do you know what's crazy? If whatever is causing the anger is addressed honestly and in a loving way, it has the ability to actually deepen and strengthen relationships.

Grateful today that God's Word helps us remember that fighting the enemy sometimes means working through our anger. As the sun goes down each day, may we have the grace and wisdom to not sin in our anger and to let it be a catalyst for honest and loving conversations that deepen relationships.

- Is there anything you've been angry about for a while?
- How have you handled that anger?
- How might you take a step toward resolving that anger before the day is done?

Father, You know the reasons I am stirred up to anger. I lay out all of those situations to You right now, and ask You to give me the strength to speak truthfully about how I feel with those I need to make amends with. I trust You to help fight the enemy by helping me weed out any anger that is sinking its roots into my heart!

The Lord is my shepherd, I shall not be in want.
He makes me lie down in green pastures, he leads
me beside quiet waters, he restores my soul.

PSALM 23:1–3A

This verse is so well known and such a beautiful promise. I have found great comfort in these words over the years, but in seasons when my heart was aching, it felt harder to believe. It felt hard to read "I shall not be in want" when my soul felt left in the dust, longing for so much, for a different outcome to the story I was walking through. Have you ever felt that way when reading promises like this in Scripture? It can be so confusing.

Sometimes seasons of "being in want" descend upon your normal from out of nowhere, and sometimes the "valley" seems like it is just where you will always live, but I can honestly say that I have known God's comfort and restoration even in those kinds of seasons. I have found that even in the valley, when God is shepherding us, our soul really does have what it needs. We are not in a state of "want" when it comes to His nearness and tenderness . . . even if our current view of the world looks dim and dark.

I wrote my song "The Valley" about this beautiful promise, begging God to help me believe that He could indeed restore my soul, even when I was walking through the valley of the shadow of death.

So come and find me in the darkest night of my soul
In the shadow of the valley, I am dying for You to make me whole
For You to make me whole.

I'm not saying that God changed my circumstances every time like I hoped He would, but He has met me in the middle of the "wanting" places and breathed hope and light and love over them. He has been able to give me rest and comfort in the midst of chaos.

He has led me beside quiet waters even in the midst of some of the biggest storms I've known in my life. If that's where you are today, in a dark valley, know that you're not the only one who has been there. My prayer is that you'll experience His comfort and rest, His presence and peace, even in the lowest parts of the journey. God, thank You that You are our gentle Shepherd, and that You know what we need, even when we're walking through the shadows.

- What is the hardest or deepest valley you've ever walked through in life? How did God bring you through that valley?

- How does that past memory give you faith and trust for whatever valley you may be traveling through today (or tomorrow)?

- How might you come alongside and encourage a friend who is in a valley right now? Take a moment to pray this verse over that friend right now.

Father, my Great Shepherd, You know the valley I face today. Help me sense Your nearness, and strengthen me with the faith to believe You are walking right beside me in nearness and comfort and love. When You lead me to green pastures, help me to rest. As you guide me beside quiet waters, help me to breathe new light and life into my weariness today. And as I walk through the valley of the shadow of death, help me to remember that You are with me.

Those who look to him are radiant; their
faces are never covered with shame.

PSALM 34:5

Have you ever faced seasons of life where you spent way too much time hiding—from God and other people? I have *been* there. I spent so many years of my life hiding, not knowing it was okay to *not* be okay. Any struggle or brokenness I had, I felt like I had to cover it up and not let anyone see. As you may well know, that was exhausting.

I love that because of what Jesus did for us, we get to come to God *just* as we are. We get to be completely known *and* completely loved at the same time. This verse in Psalm 34 reminds me of that truth—that when I look to Him, I don't have to hide; all of my shame is removed for good and no longer covers me. In fact, this has been one of my favorite verses since I was in college, and it's the anchoring verse for my song "You Are Loved." I remember wanting to write a song that could help younger girls see themselves the way God sees them, and by the end of writing the song, me and my co-writer friends were weeping because we needed to remember this powerful truth as well:

> *You are loved not because of what you've done*
> *Even when your heart has run the other way*
> *Nothing's gonna change His love*
> *You are wanted not because you are perfect*
> *I know that you don't think you're worth that kind of grace*
> *But look into His face, you'll know . . . that you are loved*

Friend, there is no room for shame in the gospel, and having lived under the weight of shame for so many years of my life, I'm so grateful for the freedom that comes with being *both* known and loved. In fact, as I continue to own the brokenness in my life more and more, the power of God's love for me becomes more and more beautiful.

I love that this verse reminds us that "those who look to him are *radiant*" (emphasis added). We have nothing to hide, no need to hustle for our worth, because our eyes are on the One who made us, the One who loves us, the One who has rescued us, and the One who will never leave us no matter what kind of messes we get ourselves into. May we ever be looking up into the eyes of Love.

- In what ways do you sometimes hide from God or others?

- Or, on the flip side, how do you try to prove yourself to God or others?

- Ask God to silence every other voice but His, and to show you how He sees you. Listen and write down what He says.

- How would your internal posture toward yourself and the world change if you believed you were both fully known and fully loved by God?

Jesus, lift my eyes to You today. As I look up to You, help me remember that Your work removed all my shame, and I don't have to hide anymore! Help me trust that in Your presence, I am both known and loved.

DAY
68

For the wages of sin is death, but the gift of God
is eternal life in Christ Jesus our Lord.

ROMANS 6:23

Have you ever gotten your heart into trouble? Maybe letting it dwell on all the wrong things some days? Or letting it lead you to actions you know you don't *actually* want for your life, but you do them anyway in a moment of exhaustion or weakness? Have you ever had to face the consequences afterward, feeling ashamed and distant from God?

I certainly have.

I get my heart into trouble so many days and know firsthand the consequences of sin in my life, so when I read and remember this verse, I'm *so* grateful for the gift God gives us. It's not something we deserve, or something we earn, but a gift—life to the full here on this earth . . . and then forever. All because we're in Christ. All because He's not so distant after all. He's paid the wages for all our sin, all our weak and tired moments, and offers us forever with Him in return. Y'all, what a gift. What a promise. What a light for us in the very moments we stumble in the darkness.

Isn't it amazing to know that when our heart is in trouble, we can remember? We can remember the gift we've been given and the forever future we have with God. We can remember He paid for—in full—whatever that thing is we did that's making us feel distant from Him. He's *promised* us this. I stumble and fall, and maybe today you know what that feels like. But what if we believed together that God still has a gift for us, one He wants us to enjoy today, tomorrow, and for eternity? It's not just the gift of forgiveness. It's the gift of life eternal, of being brought into the family of God and into the epic story of His love for us and His kingdom that's coming!

Fighting to remember this gift of life is so good for my heart today. I pray it is for you too.

- What gets your heart into trouble most these days? Why do you think that's the case?

- What consequences are you facing today, due to the moments you have stumbled? What promise does this verse speak over those decisions and consequences?

- How does it feel to know that life with God is something the Lord wants you to experience not just in eternity, but today?

Jesus, I know my sin and stumbling has a price. Thank You so much for not only paying it, but for giving me the gift of life-to-the full both here and forever in the family of God. Help me remember this is true when my heart pulls me in the wrong direction, and give me the strength to take hold of the gift You've given me in moments of weakness, weariness, or sin.

The Spirit of the Sovereign LORD is on me, because the
LORD has anointed me to proclaim good news to the poor.
He has sent me to bind up the brokenhearted, to proclaim
freedom for the captives and release from darkness for
the prisoners, to proclaim the year of the LORD's favor
and the day of vengeance of our God, to comfort all who
mourn, and provide for those who grieve in Zion—to bestow
on them a crown of beauty instead of ashes, the oil of joy
instead of mourning, and a garment of praise instead of a
spirit of despair. They will be called oaks of righteousness,
a planting of the LORD for the display of his splendor.

ISAIAH 61:1-3

It may or may not be Advent season as you are reading this, but
I have always loved Isaiah 61, especially around Christmas time. I am
so drawn to this passage because it is the prophecy of the ministry of
Jesus, and that feels so powerful to me. I am so grateful for the truth
we celebrate each year during December—that we have a Rescuer
who has come to bring us GOOD NEWS.

Jesus came to bind up the brokenhearted, and that is what I've
seen Him do over and over again in my life. December can often be
a joyful and magical time of year, but my goodness, it can be hard as
well. Whether it's another year of longings unmet or it reminds you of
people in your life who have passed and are no longer with you, the
end of the year can feel lonely and bleak to many of us.

So, I *love* that heaven's answer for our earthly brokenheartedness is Jesus, who binds us up, who frees us, who gives us a reason
to hope. The broken state of things in our hearts and our world did
not scare Him off. Instead, that's the very reason He came—to give

us comfort instead of mourning, beauty instead of ashes, and light instead of darkness! God didn't stay at a safe distance from our pain. He got close to it not only to comfort us, but to heal us and make us strong, like a sturdy tree. No matter how dark the end of the year may feel to some of us, that's certainly something to rejoice over. My song "He Will" is grounded in this powerful verse, and it is my way of reminding my soul to sing His promises into the sadness. Perhaps we can do that here together today?

> *He'll give beauty for our ashes; He'll restore the oil of gladness*
> *We will praise Him through our sadness,*
> *until the promise is fulfilled*
> *He will, He will, He will, He will*

- Is the end of the year a joyful time or a hard time for you? How so?

- How does it feel to know that Jesus is not scared off by brokenness?

- Reread today's passage. What specific part speaks to you most today? Why?

Thank You, God, for sending Your Son to rescue and restore me, and for promising to always give beauty for my ashes, which gives me a forever-reason to praise You through my sadness. Clothe me with a garment of praise today and lift my eyes to see Your face when I am tempted to lose hope. Along with others around me, grow us into "oaks of righteousness" people, rooted deeply in Your unfailing love.

Then Jesus told them this parable: "Suppose one of you
has a hundred sheep and loses one of them. Doesn't
he leave the ninety-nine in the open country and go
after the lost sheep until he finds it? And when he finds
it, he joyfully puts it on his shoulders and goes home.
Then he calls his friends and neighbors together and
says, 'Rejoice with me; I have found my lost sheep.'"

LUKE 15:3–6

I don't know about you, but I seem to lose *everything*. And most
of the time, it's no big deal. When it comes to things like the bobby
pins I swore I *just* bought at the store, the socks in our house, or
the pens in my purse, I can just shrug my shoulders and carry on if
I can't find the thing I need. Those situations are in the category of
"not the end of the world." But then there are other situations where
it matters a *whole lot* if I've lost something. For instance, my wallet.
Or heaven forbid, one of my kids. That would fall in the category of a
full-on, blare the sirens, bring in the cavalry, "definitely the end of the
world and we need to fix it right now" situation.

Whenever I come across this parable about the lost sheep, I
always tear up a bit, because reading it makes me realize that the
idea of losing us, to Jesus, would fall in the second category. From the
Lord's perspective, we aren't one bobby pin of a hundred bobby pins
to Him. We're His beloved children. And losing us isn't an option for
Him. Even if He has ninety-nine others who are right where they are
supposed to be, He will stop to go find the one who is wandering. He
will tear across the countryside and "go after the lost sheep until he
finds it." Nothing will stop Him when He senses that one of His own is
straying, all alone on the road away from Him.

If that isn't encouraging enough, it lifts my heart even more to realize that Jesus could have said "goat" here—the term He loves to use when trying to describe those who are outside of His fold. But He says "sheep"—the common symbol used for His followers. He's helping us see that wandering happens to sheep too, not just goats! We go down the wrong path, we lose our way, we forget the right road. And every single time, He leaves the ninety-nine to come after the one. He comes to find us and bring us back to safety. He "joyfully puts us on his shoulders and goes home." What a Savior, a tender Shepherd.

If you're wandering today, feeling far away from God, take heart: you may be disoriented, but *you're still a sheep!* And perk those ears up, because soon you'll hear the footsteps of your Savior joyfully running to find you. Jesus, thank You for being a Shepherd who always finds us when we lose our way, and brings us back home.

- Have you ever had a season where you wandered away from God? What was that like?

- How did He come find you?

- If there's a loved one in your life who is wandering from God, take some time to pray this passage over their life today, trusting that Jesus is running hard after them to bring them back into His loving care.

Jesus, thank You for being the kind of Savior who leaves the ninety-nine to come find me when I wander! In the moments I lose my way, help tune my ears to the steps of You running after me, and give me the faith to believe I'm still a sheep in Your beloved fold.

Trust in the LORD with all your heart and do not lean on
your own understanding. In all your ways acknowledge
Him, and He will make your paths straight.

PROVERBS 3:5–6 NASB

I don't know what you rely on when life looks confusing, and
I can't tell you why you might lean into that person or thing, but I
can tell you this: I have spent a whole lot of time trying to lean on
my own understanding in my life. I've tried turning a situation over
in my mind all day long. I've tried problem-solving and strategizing
and scenario-making and all the things that come with trusting in my
own wisdom. Maybe you've gone that route too when a curve ball
has come your way.

But God's grace to me is this: I've also tried leaning on the Lord,
trusting Him even when my eyes and my mind can't make sense of
what is going on in my life or around me. And you know what? I never
regret the time I spend acknowledging Him.

Maybe I'm alone in this, but I used to think this verse meant
that if I prayed and acknowledged God in my messes, it would make
everything work out exactly like I wanted it to. I know that's not true
now, but I also know that God is a way-maker. I've seen Him show up
in the most dire and dark circumstances to make a way from hope-
lessness to hope, from darkness to light, from fear to peace. It may
not have looked the way I wanted it to. It may not have matched one
of the scenarios I tried to forecast, but in His own time and in His own
way, somehow, He made the path straight. Time and time again, I've
walked right out of a situation that I thought I was trapped in, that I
thought had no logical way out of, but His hand holds me and guides
me through, and I can look back and see the love of God moving in
ways beyond my understanding.

He makes our path straight. He leads us in the face of the confusing or the impossible when all our best plans and strategies fall short. And all we have to do is look to Him, acknowledge Him, rest in Him. That's the kind of God we follow. I don't know what situations you need a straight path for, but I sure do have plenty. Instead of leaning into our own wisdom and understanding, let's acknowledge the Lord—the way-maker—today.

- What does "leaning into your own understanding" look like for you? Why do you think we often trust in our own strategies to solve our problems instead of acknowledging the Lord?

- In what past situations have you seen God unexpectedly make your path straight?

- Think of some circumstances you've been trying to solve all by yourself. How might you lean into trusting God's ability to make a way today instead of leaning into your own understanding?

Lord, help me to continue to acknowledge You in all my moments, so that whatever I'm facing can be eclipsed by Your deep love for me. You know the situations I carry today. I give them to You and ask You to make my path straight, in Your timing and in Your way.

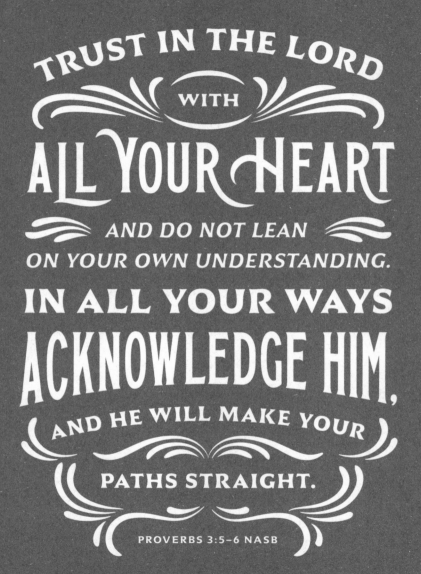

TRUST IN THE LORD WITH ALL YOUR HEART AND DO NOT LEAN ON YOUR OWN UNDERSTANDING. IN ALL YOUR WAYS ACKNOWLEDGE HIM, AND HE WILL MAKE YOUR PATHS STRAIGHT.

PROVERBS 3:5–6 NASB

DAY
72

On my bed I remember you; I think of you through
the watches of the night. Because you are my
help, I sing in the shadow of your wings.

PSALM 63:6–7

Have you ever had a restless night's sleep? I know I have. My precious mother-in-law once told me that when she is really restless at night and can't fall back asleep, she takes it as an opportunity to pray. She always says, "The Lord must be waking me up to pray for somebody who needs it, so I just lay in bed and begin lifting up whoever comes to mind."

I love that perspective so much, and I have followed her lead many a restless night. It has been so helpful to interpret what is usually a stressful situation (not being able to get back to sleep) as an invitation into prayer and conversation with God. After all, our God does not sleep. He's always awake and ready to hear us and offer us the help and comfort and peace we need. (It's also been wonderful to see who God brings to mind and often to discover later that they were in desperate need of prayer during the same times or days when God woke me up to pray for them. What a reminder to me that He sees us and supports us, and that He invites us into the beautiful work of seeing and supporting one another.)

This verse from Psalm 63 makes me think of those moments during restless nights, when instead of worrying, I am learning to shift my gaze to God, my Help, and sing or pray under the shadow of His wings. So grateful that He's always awake, even when I'm not supposed to be. *Especially* then.

I hope you sleep so well tonight, but if you don't, I hope you'll think of the Lord, your Helper, through the watches of the night.

— When you can't sleep, what sort of thoughts keep you awake?

— According to this passage, what gives us the confidence to "sing in the shadow of God's wings"?

— If you have restless moments today or tonight, who in your life might benefit if you turned those moments into opportunities for prayer?

🔥 Father, You know the reason for my restless heart today. Instead of staying isolated, alone in the dark, I come to You right now and trust that You are my help and my strong support. Thank You for being a God who is ready and waiting to uphold me and hear my cries and my songs, even through the watches of the night.

Do everything in love.

1 CORINTHIANS 16:14

I have a tendency to over-complicate things. When it comes to the best way to approach life or problems, I can easily add a thousand different well-meaning "quick tips" or "series of steps" to the pile of ideas. And then, over time, I get bogged down. I wonder which one is right. I can't remember them all. And I realize I've probably made things too hard.

This tendency in myself is why I just can't get enough of this verse in 1 Corinthians.

When in doubt? Do everything in love.

When you make a mistake? Respond to yourself in a loving way rather than a self-shaming way.

When someone else makes a mistake? Respond to that in love as well.

When we work, when we play, when we meet with friends, when we meet strangers, when we cook, when we apologize, when we face hardship, we don't need a thousand strategies or quick tips or complicated steps. We have a better way. A simple way. We can approach it all in love. Because that's the way of God.

I don't know what you are facing today. But I do know this: no matter what it is, the way forward is love. The way forward in *everything* is love.

- In what ways do you over-complicate things?
- In what situations is it natural for you to respond in love? Why?

- What situations feel unnatural for you to offer a loving response? Why?

- In what current circumstance might God be calling you past your default reactions, and to instead react in love? How can you take a step toward that today?

🔥 Lord, help me to know how to do all of life in love. I'm so thankful that You are love and that You live in me, so that I might have access to limitless love every day. Help me to open myself up first to receive Your love and then to do everything else as I am resting in Your love for me.

You will keep in perfect peace those whose minds are
steadfast, because they trust in you. Trust in the LORD
forever, for the LORD, the LORD himself, is the Rock eternal.

ISAIAH 26:3-4

I feel like my mind is anything but steadfast a lot of days. Is that
true for you too? I often feel scattered, moving ungracefully from one
thought to another. It is so easy to get distracted for me, and so I
come to these words from Isaiah, and I'm reminded that generally
when I am feeling scattered and split in every direction, it's because
I'm putting my trust and my hope in things that will never truly offer
me rest or measure up to the Lord and His love for me.

Maybe you've been there too. Instead of focusing on a really big
God, our attention ping-pongs between a million little things throughout the day. We open our eyes, and just from the bed to bathroom
to the breakfast table to the front door, we've already had hundreds
of thoughts. *I should make the bed. I need new mascara—add it to the
list. Did I switch out the laundry for the kids' clothes today? This coffee
pot needs cleaning. So do those toys—I thought I told them to pick that
up! What happened to the creamer? Add it to the list too. I'm behind on
that text thread from yesterday; I should text them back. Where are my
keys again?*

Or maybe on certain days, our attention isn't scattered as much
as it is hyper-focused on the wrong things. We see something about
our body we want to change as we get ready in the morning, and
we dwell on it all day long. We had an unexpected disagreement
with a friend or spouse, and we replay the conversation in our head
from morning till night, zoning out to all other conversations God
might have for us to engage in. We experience a financial blow that

consumes our thoughts, even into the night, stealing our sleep and sanity. Our mind is steadfast, yes, but not toward God.

So in the midst of our busy, stressed, scattered, or consuming seasons—whether they be full of "to-do" lists, preparations for celebrations, holiday planning, grocery runs, work emails, diaper changes, constant advertisements of things we "need," figuring out dinner, dealing with a crisis, or just getting the kids to do their home-work on time, may we remember that God gives perfect peace to those who trust in Him. A million things on my plate or not, may we rest in Him before we go about our doing, and find sure footing and perfect peace on the Rock of Salvation. He is always steadfast, even when we aren't. He is always trustworthy, even when we forget.

- Do you tend to be scattered in your thinking, or hyper-focused?

- What things does your mind tend to dwell on? Why?

- Do you believe God is strong enough to help you focus your mind on Him and trust Him? How might your experience of peace change if you lived into that belief on a daily basis?

God, thank You that even when I am not steadfast, YOU always are, and You stand at the ready to help us keep our mind on You and also offer us Your perfect peace. I trust You today with all my scattered thoughts, and I open myself up to receive the peace You promise me!

Your unfailing love, O LORD, is as vast as the heavens;
your faithfulness reaches beyond the clouds.

PSALM 36:5 NLT

Where do you go when you need a little perspective? For me, I love the perspective I always gain from being with my kids and other children. They help me see the world like new again.

My sweet three-year-old son loves planes and trains and trucks. So now when I see a plane or train or truck, I get excited like a kid again—even if he's not there with me—just because I know he loves those things. My favorite thing that he says when he sees a jet is this: "Mom!! A JET! Way way high, high up in the sky." He spotted three jets yesterday, and his sweet words came to mind when I read this verse.

God's love is *big*—bigger and farther and vaster than the heavens. Or, in the words of our little family, it's "way, way high, high up in the sky." His faithfulness soars above the clouds and the atmosphere. There's no amount of mistakes or trouble or brokenness that is too much to be covered and healed by His love and mercy. They are in limitless supply.

I don't know about you, but I'm banking on that truth today, because I've made my fair share of mistakes this week, and I'm so grateful that even when I screw it all up, God's love and faithfulness still reach way high up in the sky for me and for you.

- Why do you think we sometimes treat God's love and faithfulness like they are in short supply?

- How does it encourage you to know that God's love and faithfulness are so big and vast that they can't run out?

- How would you put this verse in your own words?

Lord, thank You that Your love and faithfulness are not only big, but limitless! I run to You today, and I ask You again to fill me up with Your love. Give me eyes to see all the ways You are being faithful to me, and help me lean into You when I'm tempted to believe the lie that You don't have enough love to give.

"I will not leave you as orphans; I will come to you."

JOHN 14:18

In His final teachings and encouragements to His disciples before His arrest, Jesus makes some powerful promises. One of them is right here in verse 8—"I will come to you." I'm so grateful for this promise.

What a relief to know that God's desire is to be close to us. He doesn't stand at a distance and shake His head at our shortcomings; He sent His Son to be one of us, so we could know who He is and how He loves us. It's amazing to stop and think about that, isn't it? Jesus didn't stay away. Instead, He came to us. That's His heart—one that wants to draw near. And we can be sure of that because Scripture shows us that He kept this promise when He came to earth. *And* He kept this promise when He appeared to His followers after His resurrection. *And* He kept this promise *again* when the Holy Spirit came to live in us. And on top of all that, He will keep this promise when He returns to finally and fully restore a broken world! This is a promise that we've seen Him fulfill over and over, which means we can take it to the bank again and again.

If you've ever had days when you feel abandoned, take heart, God has come to you. He will never cast you off like an orphan. He wraps His arms around you as His very own child. And this is not a burden for Him; it's His deepest desire! It's what He *loves* to do. So let's draw near to the One drawing near to us today. Let's believe this promise together as we face whatever our day holds.

- Why do you think we sometimes assume that God's instinct would be to withdraw or recoil from us instead of coming close?

- Can you think of any examples in Scripture where God comes near His people? List them below.

- How does this list encourage you today? How does it challenge your assumption that God would want to leave you as an orphan?

Lord, help me be quick to remember that You don't leave us or abandon us. You come to us, and I can come to You as I am with all of my mess because in Christ, I am Your beloved child.

DAY
77

The heavens declare the glory of God; the skies proclaim
the work of his hands. Day after day they pour forth
speech; night after night they reveal knowledge.
They have no speech, they use no words; no sound
is heard from them. Yet their voice goes out into all
the earth, their words to the ends of the world.

PSALM 19:1–4

I can't tell you how many times the stars have reminded me of God's love and light. There have been countless nights when I have shaken my fist at the heavens asking God, "Why?!" There have been other nights I've been too drained or lonely or defeated to even muster up a fist to shake in the first place.

I'll never forget the night my dad showed me how to find the Northern Cross constellation. We were visiting our family at the ranch in Texas that my grandmother grew up on, and because this little ranch is in the middle of nowhere with little to no ambient light, the stars are majestic. After pointing it out to me, he told me that there had been many nights in his life when he felt lost and alone, but somehow he'd end up looking up to the sky and finding the Northern Cross, which helped him remember that no matter how broken he was feeling in the moment, that Jesus was broken for him so he could know that he would never face any heartache alone. Ever since then, almost every time I have been in one of those desperate places in the night, I look to the sky and encounter the stars and the Northern Cross, shining bravely in the dark, reminding me that no matter how dark the night gets, God's love and light will be with me.

Taken together, that memory of my dad's advice and this verse in Psalm 19 stirred me to write a song called "Constellations." These are the lyrics from the bridge of the song:

When I felt the light of the moon on my face, the
memory of sun that'd been shining for days
You've already been in this desolate place
You've already been here and You've made a way
Pinpricks of glory strung out across the sky,
Memories of darkness undone by the light
Reminding me You are right here by my side
You're here by my side, You're here by my side

When you see the stars tonight, let them tell you something about the light and beauty of Christ. Let them remind you that no matter how defeated or bleak your life may feel, there is hope even in our darkest nights, and morning will always come! Lord, thank You for reminding us of this truth over and over again, as we look to the heavens.

- What sensation are you filled with when you look to the sky at night?

- What typically distracts you from lifting your eyes to what God might teach you about Himself in creation?

- If not the sky, do you have a favorite spectacle in nature that reminds you of the truth? What is it? And what about God's character does it help you remember?

🔥 God, thank You for creating the sky with such care, beauty, creativity, and wonder. Thank You for reminding me who You are through the world You've made. In the moments my gaze drops in exhaustion or frustration, lift my head, and help me sense Your light and love nearby.

Jesus stood and said in a loud voice, "Let anyone
who is thirsty come to me and drink. Whoever
believes in me, as Scripture has said, rivers of
living water will flow from within them."

JOHN 7:37–38

Have you ever been *really* thirsty? Maybe when you were on a hike and forgot your water bottle? Or as a kid, when you were playing outside on a hot summer day, you'd run inside, throw the water faucet on, and take a long drink straight from the sink. I can recall only a few times in my life when I didn't have access to water; and when I finally did get to drink, it was the most wonderful and satisfying thing!

We've all been physically thirsty. But what about emotionally or spiritually? Are you thirsty in those places? Wanting more from this life than it's been giving you? I've felt that way too, and you know what has encouraged me lately? The fact that God knows we were made to desire deep things—the deepest of all being Him, and He knows that anything we might use to try and satisfy that desire will never satisfy us like His love. He knows we'll be thirsty for more in this life when we put our faith, trust, and love in other things besides Him, and so He tells us to come to *Him* before we come to anything else. Isn't it amazing to think that God *wants* us to be satisfied? That He directs us to Himself not only to bring Himself glory, but also to ensure our thirst is fully quenched? What a reason to love Him!

Yet, so many days I have to re-order my "loves."[3] I put other things in front of Jesus, thinking they will satisfy or complete me. Have you ever done that? It encourages me to know that Jesus knows I am tempted to do this, and that He helps me place Himself back at the front of the line with the promise that in the very places my other loves fail me, *He* stands ready to fill me up with rivers of living water when I simply believe. He stands ready to quench my thirst in the most wonderful and satisfying way.

Let's ask Him to help us re-order our loves today. Let's remember He offers us Himself to fill us up so that our wells will never run dry. Let's ask Him to help us believe today and every day that He is the One true lover of our souls, the only one who truly satisfies, and the source of all life and goodness, and may we be the kind of people who have rivers of living water flowing from within!

- In what ways are you "thirsty" today?
- Where do you typically run to quench this thirst?
- When your heart starts getting the things it loves out of order, what usually rises to the top above Jesus?
- What are some practical ways you can you drink deeply from the rivers of living water Jesus offers you today?

Jesus, I ask You to help me believe today, so that I can drink deeply from the wells of Your love and be a conduit for those rivers of living water. Re-order my loves, I pray, and help me run to You when I am thirsty.

DAY
79

"Assemble the people, men, women, and little ones,
and the sojourner within your towns, that they may
hear and learn to fear the LORD your God . . ."

DEUTERONOMY 31:12 ESV

When you see the command to "fear God" in Scripture, does it feel confusing to you? It did to me for so many years. Why be scared of a Lord who came to save us—to the point of dying for us? Why be terrified of the One who wants us to know Him as a loving Father? Why fear Him if "perfect love casts out fear"?

My confusion was lifted when I learned that "fearing God," for believers, doesn't mean we should feel nothing but terror in His presence. Instead, it simply means we are awestruck by Him and we give Him the most weight in our life compared to other things. We value Him and what He says more than we value any other thing or what anyone else says.

I'm thankful the Bible doesn't just tell us to do this, but shows us how in the lives of ordinary people in the Bible. For example, I think of the Hebrew midwives who were commanded by Pharoah to kill all the male Israelite babies. When faced with this terrible situation, "the midwives, however, *feared* God and did not do what the king of Egypt had told them to do; they let the boys live" (Exod. 1:17, emphasis added). In a moment of crisis, these brave women gave more weight to what God thought than what Pharoah thought, and in doing so, saved a whole generation of kids!

May we walk forward today in that kind of conviction—that our God holds the most weight in our life, and that we need not fear anyone else!

- How have you typically defined "the fear of the Lord"?

- In what ways have you seen it turn out for good when you prioritized God's opinion over the opinion of others?

- If you are struggling to give God the most weight in your life today, take some time to pray that He would instill awe and wonder in your heart toward Him.

God, You deserve the most weight in my life, and I pray You'll help me put Your opinion above every other opinion. In the moments I get distracted from the awe and wonder I should have over You, restore these things in me, and help me fear Your name!

God is not unjust; he will not forget your work
and the love you have shown him as you have
helped his people and continue to help them.

HEBREWS 6:10

I just cannot get over this promise! So many days, our work goes unseen, or it least it feels that way to me. I don't know what it looks like for you—maybe it's changing diapers or cleaning up after a worship service or serving to your sick friend or laboring hard in whatever job you currently have.

It's so hard in these moments to not get discouraged. If you're anything like me, after so many thankless hours of service and work in the shadows, you just want to throw in the towel. You wonder if anyone even cares, or if anyone is even really being helped. You wonder if *God* even sees.

Falling right smack-dab in the middle of that exhaustion is this promise—no matter how it looks, and no matter how long the days are or how thankless it seems, God doesn't forget our work! He sees it. He takes note. He values it. Another translation puts it this way: "God is not unjust so as to overlook your work and the love that you have shown for his name" (ESV).

God doesn't overlook your labor, friend. It might be in the shadows to others, but it's plain as day, in the light, to Him. He knows the hours you toil and love you have for His name, and He recognizes it, even now. Lord, thank You for seeing the work that goes on behind the scenes. Thank You for being a God who cares about all the small and big ways we serve You and Your people. Give us hearts to continue serving You, knowing that You see and You care.

- What work have you been doing in God's name that feels thankless?

- When you sense that your work is going unseen by others, how do you usually respond?

- Who in your life is doing a lot of good work in the name of the Lord? How might you come alongside and encourage that person?

Father, I thank You for being a God who overlooks nothing—there's not one moment of labor You do not see in my life and treasure dearly. In the moments I resent doing a thankless task in the shadows for Your name or for Your people, help me remember it's not in the shadows to You!

For God has not given us a spirit of fear, but
of power, of love, and of a sound mind.

2 TIMOTHY 1:7 NKJV

I told you in another devotional about my daughter—how she would sometimes fear the shadows in her room or the threat of monsters under her bed when she was younger. As I said before, we memorized a little verse in Isaiah to help with the fear. Since then, we have taken up yet another verse to help us when we are afraid. This promise in 2 Timothy, has been a powerful tool to hold on to as the Tennessee thunderstorms roll through our state in the spring, especially after surviving the EF4 tornado that destroyed so much of our neighborhood just over a year ago. As the thunder pounds, the winds knock over trees, and the rain and hail *pour* out of the sky, we have literally been singing this verse into the storms.

I looked up what the word *spirit* meant when my girl asked about it, and while there are many ways this word can be interpreted, it seems that this gets at the heart of what it might mean here:

"the rational spirit, the power by which a human
being feels, thinks, wills, decides."[4]

I love that God doesn't just say He wants us to move about our days and trials unafraid. Instead, He gives us something to replace the fear with: a spirit of power, of love, and of a sound mind. The power of the One who raised the dead lives within us. The love of the One who gave everything to defeat death and brokenness so we could draw near to God surrounds us. When you look up the phrase "a sound mind" in Greek (which is the language this verse was originally written in), it means a "self-controlled" mind. That means that God has given us the ability to restrain and redirect our thoughts.

When they have settled on things that are scary, we have the power to turn them away from fear, and toward Him. (I want to whisper here that I know full well that there are certainly mental illnesses that make a simple task like this one of redirecting your heart toward the truth seem like throwing tiny drops of water on a fire. While I do truly believe that this exercise of redirecting our thoughts will help us no matter where we are or what we are walking through, I also believe that God gives us medicine and counselors and doctors to help us navigate how to have healthy and sound minds, and strongly encourage using all of these resources when necessary.)

I take such heart with all of this because even when we are afraid, this verse reminds me that we have a choice in which way we want our minds to go. We can let fear cripple us, or we can lean into the power and love of Jesus, and trust that He will help us have the self-control to look at Him rather than at our circumstances. If we can shift our eyes from the thing that scares the daylights out of us to the One who descended down to hell and then walked out of a grave, we begin to have courage. We remember that whatever we are scared of, no matter how intense it may be, is not stronger than Him. How great is our God that He gives us the option and the power to live this way?

- What are some consistent thought-struggles you've faced lately?

- In what ways have you treated the things you fear as if they are stronger than Jesus?

- How might God be asking you to restrain or redirect your thoughts today, away from fear and toward Him?

🕯 Lord, thank You that You don't give us fear, but love and power and self-control. Help me to walk in faith with my eyes fixed on You, and when I am tempted to look away or entertain fearful thinking, give me the power to remain in Your strength and hold on to Your promises.

FOR GOD HAS NOT GIVEN US A SPIRIT OF FEAR

BUT OF POWER, OF LOVE, AND OF A SOUND MIND.

2 TIMOTHY 1:7 NKJV

DAY
82

The LORD is near to the brokenhearted
and saves the crushed in spirit.

PSALM 34:18

I don't know what brokenheartedness has looked like for you. Maybe it's the loss of a loved one. Maybe it's the betrayal of a friend. Maybe it's the unfulfilled dreams for a husband or a baby or a job. Maybe it's a horrible diagnosis. Maybe it's some shattered dream that only you know about, deep in the recesses of your soul. Whatever it looks like, a broken heart is crushing, even debilitating, when we bear it alone. When our spirit has been broken, we can't seem to face the day. We can't wake up enough to engage. We have a hard time mustering up the energy to get even the simplest of tasks done. We're lost in a fog that seems like it will go on forever.

One thing I love about the Bible is that it doesn't try to skip over this sort of suffering. Scripture acknowledges—and at times *guarantees*—that we will experience a broken heart. And the wildest part is that try as the enemy might to convince us otherwise, God doesn't run away from all that heartbreak. He comes close to it. I suppose that makes sense when I remember He's a heavenly Father to us. Even in my own flawed parenting, I don't want to run away from my kids when they are crestfallen, but instead, I reflexively scoop them up in my arms as their tears fall down. I want to hold them. I want to take the pain away—to save them in any way I can. I can't always spare them from the difficulties of life, but nothing will stop me from reaching toward them in the midst of their pain because I love them.

Earthly parenting is just a shadow of the way God does it—which means that to whatever extent I feel this impulse to scoop up my own kids when they're heartbroken, God's impulse is a million times stronger! Let that truth sweep over you—no matter how deep the heartbreak, God's nearness, His radiant love, His warm compassion, and His sturdy promises go deeper still.

If you are brokenhearted today, or if you feel that your spirit is crushed by the weight of all the pain you're experiencing, take heart. The lies of the enemy will tell you that God is far away. He isn't! He wants to scoop you up, right in the middle of the pain.

- Which lies of the enemy have tried to mislead you in past seasons of pain? Which ones did you believe?

- What experience has crushed you in spirit recently? Where did you run for comfort? Why?

- How does it feel to know that when God sees you in the middle of heartbreak, His impulse isn't to run away, but scoop you up?

🔥 Lord, thank You for being a God who is not far off from pain, but understands it deeply, and can walk through it with me in empathy and compassion. Give me the strength to believe that when I'm in that place of brokenheartedness, as a good Father, You rush in to scoop me up and love on me.

DAY
83

But we have this treasure in jars of clay to show that this
all-surpassing power is from God and not from us.

2 CORINTHIANS 4:7

If there's any verse that reminds me that God doesn't need us to be perfect or grand or beautiful or talented to use us, it's this one. Truth? I have felt like not enough a lot of days. I keep trying to do too much and feeling like I'm failing at all the things. Does that ever happen to you? Like you spin your wheels over and over, and for all your striving, you just don't feel like you get anywhere?

That happened to me recently—last week I was trying to get an album finished, plan out some special family time for our kids, rehearse for a live-streamed event for a collaborative project I was a part of, and also get some writing and editing done on this book. By the end of the week, I felt like I just couldn't quite keep all the plates spinning. Honestly, I felt like I was drowning. I was trying to operate in my own power, not God's. I was trying to act like I had no limitations, but I do! I felt so unqualified to do the things God was calling me to do. I wanted to do it all excellently, and I wanted to look like superwoman while doing it. But no matter how hard I tried, I just couldn't.

When I read through this verse, I was reminded that God doesn't require us to be enough. He has more than enough to pour into us each day. Each moment. We mainly just need to be open to receiving His power, letting it flow through us. Why? Because we are not trophies designed for display. We're jars . . . carriers and conduits of His light and His gospel and His love. In fact, I think the more unqualified we are to do the things He calls us to do the better . . . that way He gets all the credit.

This verse also makes me think back to a season in college when I was trying to do way too many things at once . . . I wanted to make straight A's, work a side job, and be as social as I possibly could, all while taking on a leadership role in a student organization and participating in the gospel choir as well as three other student ministry groups. I think I had at least one to three events or meetings and hangs *a night*! I was dropping balls all over the place. My grades were suffering, and I was worn out. I'll never forget my dad listening to my discouraged and weary heart and then speaking this over me:

"A jar without cracks might look prettier, but when the water pours into that perfect jar, it can only come out of the top. That's all good and well, but a jar with a ton of cracks? Water is going to pour out all over the place! Embrace your cracks and the broken parts of your heart and your life, Ellie. Your cracks are where God's living water will pour through the most powerfully. Your broken heart will be what ends up helping others see Jesus more clearly and feel less alone as they find their way through this broken world."

I'm so grateful we're not confined to a shelf for others to admire how perfect we are . . . instead, we get to be conduits of God's power, grace, and love, built for community and the common good. I'm so grateful we have a source of power that doesn't end with our limited gifts and strengths. It is limitless, and we have the great joy of carrying that love and power and peace and light of God out into this weary world.

- Have you ever seen God use you as a conduit before? What was that like?

- In what ways do you feel "unqualified" in the things God has called you to? How does this verse speak to that feeling?

- In what ways might you need to stop trying to operate in your own power, and let God's all-surpassing power pour into you?

🔥 Lord, the next time I feel like I'm cracked and far from perfect, help me remember that You never meant for me to do everything on my own anyway! Thank You even though my energy, my patience, and my time all run out, Your gospel, Your love, Your mercy, and Your power never do. Let these things pour out of me today, especially from my broken places.

Let the word of Christ dwell in you richly as you teach
and admonish one another with all wisdom . . .

COLOSSIANS 3:16

I have seen such beauty grow in my heart and soul when I choose to meditate on the truth and promises that are in God's Word. When I started memorizing Scripture almost a decade ago with my friend, I began to get a new understanding of what "letting the word of Christ dwell in you richly" meant. Scripture memory is so hard, but as we made an effort to commit God's promises to memory, it started sinking in deeper, giving us access to comfort, hope, light, and truth even in our darkest hours. I hope you've had a chance to memorize some of the verses we've looked at in this book. If you have, you know what I'm talking about, and if you haven't, don't worry! It's never too late to start letting God's Word take residence in your heart!

I've loved memorizing Scripture all these years, but this is the verse that gave me the idea to start writing Scripture into songs. There's a lot I can't remember these days—but I *can* remember songs! And how beautiful is it that God doesn't just permit us to do something like that as a mere tool for memory—He actually *wants* us to sing Him songs! He knows it's good for us and He *loves* to hear our voices raised to Him, remembering the truth, and resting in gratitude.

I don't know about you, but for me, it isn't enough to just acknowledge the lies that float around in my head. I desperately need to hold on to what is *true*. And as I sing songs based on God's Word, or hide the promises of Scripture in my heart some other way, that's exactly what happens—my heart starts to move from rehearsing the truth to *believing* it, and all the untrue things start to dissipate.

Beyond this verse pointing out how wonderful it is to sing the truth, I love that it includes a "we" mentality. I'm so grateful for this part of the passage, because so often I need others to remind me of the truth. There are days I forget, days other voices seem louder than His, days I am foggy on all that God has spoken over me and about me. Sometimes we all need a friend to come alongside and "teach and admonish us with all wisdom," so that we can remember again.

What a kind God we serve, who points us to songs, gratitude, and truth—and to friends who remind us of it when we forget!

- What practices seem to work for you as you seek to "let the word of Christ dwell in you richly"?

- What sometimes holds you back from memorizing God's Word?

- What benefits have you experienced, or might you experience, from memorizing Scripture?

- Who in your life do you trust to help you remember the truth on the days you get foggy? If you don't have a friend like this, how might you take a step to cultivate a friendship like this in your life?

Jesus, please give me creative ideas today on how I might better let Your Word dwell in me. Help me remember Your truth, and lead me to a friend who might help me remember in the moments I forget.

Love is patient, love is kind. It does not envy, it does
not boast, it is not proud. It does not dishonor others,
it is not self-seeking, it is not easily angered, it keeps
no record of wrongs. Love does not delight in evil but
rejoices with the truth. It always protects, always trusts,
always hopes, always perseveres. Love never fails . . .

1 CORINTHIANS 13:4–8

Have you ever set out to memorize a verse, only for it to seriously convict you along the way as you committed it to memory? Me
too. In fact, this passage was one of the first verses I memorized, and
man . . . it punched me in the gut!

As I committed these words to memory, I kept thinking about all
the ways that I do not love very well. It was a beautiful challenge for
me to continue asking God to change my heart to make me more like
Him, and then it hit me . . . GOD is LOVE. He is *all* of these things for
us. *He* is patient, kind, humble, honoring, selfless, not easily angered,
and keeps no record of wrongs. *He* rejoices with the truth, always
protects us, always loves us. *He* is always trustworthy. *He* always
gives us good reason to hope, and *His* love will always persevere.
Love will never fail us because *God* will never fail us!

This was a huge revelation for me. I fail to measure up to this
standard of love all the time, but when I remember that this is how
God loves us, it begins to transform me and gives me the courage to
love even when it feels like it costs me something. He doesn't ask me
to do something He's never done. When it comes to love, He goes
before me. He walks in the way of love toward me, showing me what
love is like, before He ever asks me to do the same toward *others*.

May we remember today that God's love has gone before us and
never fails us, and because of this truth, may we be emboldened to

live lives surrendered to loving the people around us. Even when it's hard, even when we disagree, may we all be transformed and shaped by the power of God, who is Love. I wrote a song based on this verse called "Love Never Fails" to help me remember this beautiful truth. I'll end today with my heart's cry from the chorus of that song:

Love never fails, and that's a promise
Love never fails, help me believe it
Help me to trust that this is true, help me to love like You do
Oh, Lord, help me to live like love never fails.

— Re-read 1 Corinthians 13:4–8 above. Of this list of characteristics, which do you struggle to believe God is toward you? Why?

— Which of these characteristics do you feel like you are strong in? Weak in?

— Who in your life do you tend to disagree with often? How does this passage speak to that relationship?

🔥 Lord, thank You for being a God whose character is pure love. Thank You for always being kind and protective, and for never, ever failing me. Thank You for showing me the way of love and shaping me by the power of Your love—strengthen me to walk in that love today toward others. Help me to live like Love never fails.

But I will sing of your strength in the morning. I will sing
of your love. For you are my fortress, my refuge in times
of trouble. You are my strength, I sing praise to you;
you, God are my fortress, my God on whom I can rely.

PSALM 59:16–17

I'm sure you remember that David writes this psalm in the middle
of serious angst. Saul had sent men to watch David's house in order
to kill him; and in this moment, David is now surrounded by those
very men. He is pleading with God earlier in the psalm for rescue, but
I love that these two verses are how he ends this prayer. Even in the
midst of intense stress, David manages to sing praise to God, who is
his strength.

When I think about it, David's not the only one we see doing this
in Scripture. In Acts 16, Paul and Silas do this too when they are in
prison, remember? In the very moment their enemies surround them
and then lock them in jail, in the very moment they desperately need
rescue, they start belting out praises to God (Acts 16:22–25)!

Maybe you're in the same place today, feeling surrounded by
trouble, overwhelmed by life, or in over your head. Perhaps you feel
like you've lost any reason to lift up your voice to the Lord. Maybe
you feel like there's nothing left to rely on. I've been there too, and I
will likely be there again.

Together, we can be thankful that no matter what we face and
no matter what we might be surrounded by, we have a reason to
offer up a praise to God. Everything else may have broken down at
this point, but *He* is our strength and our refuge. He's still standing.
He's still strong enough, no matter what is closing in around us. Pour

out your heart to Him; I know I need to today. He is our God, "on whom we can rely."

- — What do you feel "surrounded by" today? What situation has made you feel like you're in over your head?
- — How has this situation altered your view of God?
- — There are psalms where David ends his prayers in despair and lament, and I'm so grateful there is room for that for us too on the days we need it, but what might be gained in ending a desperate prayer for rescue with praise? Have you ever tried that, and if so, what was your experience like?

🔥 Lord, today, as I face all manner of trials and trouble and stress, help me lean into and rely on Your goodness and faithfulness. Help me remember that You are my refuge in this situation, and that I can sing to You in the face of anything. Help me lift up a praise of Your goodness, even now.

The apostles returned to Jesus from their ministry tour
and told him all they had done and taught. Then Jesus said,
"Let's go off by ourselves to a quiet place and rest awhile."
He said this because there were so many people coming
and going that Jesus and his apostles didn't even have time
to eat. So they left by boat for a quiet place, where they
could be alone. But many people recognized them and
saw them leaving, and people from many towns ran ahead
along the shore and got there ahead of them. Jesus saw
the huge crowd as he stepped from the boat, and he had
compassion on them because they were like sheep without
a shepherd. So he began teaching them many things.

MARK 6:30–34 NLT

I'm sure every single one of us has a pet peeve that makes us a little
crazy. Want to know one of mine? Interruptions. Whether it's another
email in the inbox I have to get to, a text with an urgent message that
demands my response, or a kiddo screaming "Moooooom!" for the
seventy-fifth time in five minutes, it seems like disruptions are *especially* frequent when I'm trying to knock out something important.
And since I struggle with this, I sometimes assume God might hate
interruptions too. But when I recently considered some passages in
the book of Mark, I realized something: Jesus is so interruptible!

Just before this scene in Mark 6 takes place, Jesus was making His
way through His ministry in Galilee, and crowds were pressing in on
Him. In the middle of the flurry, a man named Jairus disrupts Jesus'
journey, and falls at His feet on behalf of his daughter, who was very
sick and in need of healing. What was our Savior's response? Was it

"give me a couple days to finish out my current plans, and I'll get back to you?" Nope. Instead we see this: "So Jesus went with him" (Mark 5:24). If that weren't amazing enough, while He's taking steps with Jairus to get to the sick little girl, Jesus is disrupted again. This time, by a woman who suffered from an issue of bleeding. She, too, begged Him for help. And you know what? He stopped what He was doing with Jairus to recognize her great faith in front of the crowds (Mark 5:32–34). While it's incredible that both the little girl and the woman end up healed in these stories, what amazes me most is this: both of these stories are interruptions on Jesus' journey, and He takes plenty of time for both.

After all that, we get our passage for today in Mark 6. It's no wonder Jesus tells His disciples they need to hop on a boat to pull away and rest awhile—their long days of ministry had clearly been full of meeting people's needs! Yet again, on His way toward the boat, Jesus is stopped by a huge crowd, and when He saw their panic and need, He "had compassion on them, because they were like sheep without a shepherd" (v. 34). They needed direction, so He paused and taught them. That's our Savior—always willing to stop and help and comfort and give us what we need.

In those moments we're tempted to think Jesus has no time for us, or that He's annoyed with our constant interruptions as we fling up yet another request or need to heaven, let's lean into what God's Word shows us about Him. Let's remember that our Savior is not in a hurry. He's not pushing us to get to our point faster or shooing us out the door on the way to His next appointment. When we flag Him down, instead of constantly checking His watch, our Jesus is ready to hear, eager to open the door at the first sound of our unexpected knock. If we go to Him, Jesus is all ears. Every time. He's happy to be interrupted by you and by me! Praying today we'll remember this truth, and that we'll let Christ's example compel us to be interruptible ourselves.

- What are some ways you regularly experience interruptions? How do you handle them?

- Have you ever gone to Jesus in fear that He'll be annoyed with you? Why?

- What might change in your relationship with God if you truly believed He wanted to stop and give you attention any time you needed it?

Jesus, thank You for wanting me to come to You in any moment, for any reason. In the moments I am tempted to think You are annoyed at my presence or too busy to spend time hearing me out, help me remember You welcome interruptions, and make me more like You in this way toward others.

The light shines in the darkness, And the
darkness has not overcome it.

JOHN 1:5

I don't know about you, but in light of the various tragedies that
have taken place all across our country in the past few years, my
heart has been so heavy. The darkness and fear in the wake of life
lost seems so strong, and understandably so. I'm not sure which
tragedy has hit you closest to home. Maybe it was the various
shootings. Maybe it was one of the natural disasters. Maybe it was
the urgent reality of our deep need for racial reconciliation in our
country. Maybe it was the global pandemic. Whatever form it took,
I'm sure you remember exactly where you were and what you were
doing when you realized what was going on. I know for me, I can
remember so many moments over the past few years that felt full of
sorrow, hopeless, devoid of light, devoid of the healing I long to see
take place.

It all seems so heavy, doesn't it? But recently, I was reminded in
this beautiful verse that even as we grieve, even on the days that feel
so dark and so broken, light is always stronger than darkness. There
is no darkness that God's love and light cannot overcome. How do
we know that? Because we serve a Savior who understands what
darkness feels like—He went through it on the cross, the greatest
tragedy of all. Yet He overcame it in glory—the resurrection. In the
darkest of situations, light and life broke in.

Today, I'm asking God to shine His light and love and comfort
into the broken hearts of all affected by these tragedies. Would you
join me? May we be a people who do not give way to fear and hate,
but live a better story as we follow in the steps of our Rescuer, Jesus.
May we go to Him when we feel the darkness rolling in, may we trust

Him to shine light in that dark place, and may we act like Him, too, reflecting His light everywhere we go to the people who need it most.

— Which recent tragedy has impacted you most? How have you coped with it?

— How does Jesus' experience of darkness and tragedy help you as you continue to move through both the pain and grief?

— How might God want to use you to show up and reflect His light into the darkness that other people are facing right now?

🔥 Lord, You know how deep my sadness goes over the tragedies we have faced as a nation and a globe recently. Help me believe again that there's no darkness that can overcome Your light. Instead of giving way to fear, strengthen me to hold on to You and to reflect Your love and light to others in this sorrowful place.

DAY
89

You are my hiding place; you will protect me from
trouble and surround me with songs of deliverance.

PSALM 32:7

Have you ever felt like you needed a place to hide, a place to
rest and be protected from all the hurt and harm that has been surrounding you? I certainly have. I can recall nights in the past when I
felt completely overwhelmed with hurt and shame and sadness, and
even in those places when I have felt so under attack, I've encountered the beautiful protection of the Lord, like a shield or covering
over me.

I'm so grateful that even in the midst of some of our most
troublesome nights, we can tuck ourselves under the Lord's strong
protection and love for us. We can trust that He will surround us
with songs of deliverance. Isn't that interesting? Of all the images the
psalmist could have used to help us visualize the protection of God,
he uses "songs of deliverance," *songs* to surround us, to hide us from
the storm, and to shield us from trouble. What a picture! Fittingly
enough, I wrote a song about all of this with my dear friend Jillian
Edwards, so I'll leave you with some lyrics from that song.

When trouble haunted me,
I heard You sing songs of deliverance.
Exposed and left ashamed,
You took me in, hid me in Your strong hands.

So when the siren sounds, I'll look to You.
I know You'll come around.
And when these waters rise.
I'll call to You, I know You'll hear my cries.

And there in my weakest hour, You offered grace.
You gave me love unfailing.
So in my heart I'll raise a banner high, to
remember how You saved me.

- Let's "raise a banner high" in our hearts today to remember God's faithfulness by writing down a story of how God has hidden you under His strong protection during past seasons of trouble.

- What kinds of lies tempt you to believe that that same protection isn't available in your current moment?

- In the face of those lies, how can you fight to remind yourself of the truth?

Lord, You know why I seek a place to hide today. You know why I need a shield and a safe place to rest. I pray You'll enable me to sense Your presence and protection right now. I cry out to You for help and safety, and I trust that even right now, You are surrounding me with songs of deliverance.

"As the Father has loved me, so I have
loved you. Now remain in my love."

JOHN 15:9

There are so many wonderful things we could pull from this verse. But today, what jumps out to me is this: Remain.

The definition of *remain* means to "stay put." What an image— one that makes me think of my kiddos. So many days I just want to sit there and hold them and love them for a moment, but they have a hard time being still in my affections. They are ready to get going, off to the next thing. Staying put isn't a concept that's easy for a kid! And I'm not just picking on them. This is true for me too! I can be just as allergic to this idea as they are! As a person who is almost always *going*, it is so easy for me to get swept up into the social/work/family shuffle, and to not think once about leaning on Jesus. I tend to do things in my own strength and then burn out, so I love this reminder to simply *remain* in God's love.

And did you catch the level to which Jesus loves us? To the level the Father loves *Him*! Think of that. Think of the depth at which the Father loves, cherishes, values, delights in, listens to, and favors His own Son. That's the exact same depth to which Jesus loves *you*. What a promise.

If I can rest there, if I can stay in God's love for me, even as I move about my days, it changes everything. So thankful today that we know how God loves us because of the way Jesus loved everyone He encountered. Grateful too for the call to simply stay put in that love. We don't have to hustle or perform. We simply have to revel in His affection for us, and let that nourish and inform all the moments of our days.

- Why is it hard for you to "stay put" in God's love for you? What tempts you to leave it?

- How does it change things to know the level to which Jesus loves you?

- What practices might help you remain in God's affections for you a little longer?

Lord, help me to remain in Your love today and all of my days. Give me eyes to see when I'm forgetting to stay put, and grant me the strength to return to Your presence and affection for me.

DAY
91

Therefore, there is now no condemnation
for those who are in Christ Jesus.

ROMANS 8:1

This is one of my favorite truths in Scripture. What a promise. No condemnation! None. Because of how Jesus broke for us, we can be certain that all of our sin has been dealt with. Our penalty is paid. Our debt is done with. All our failures and missteps and shame, taken away by the Savior who bore it for us so we wouldn't have to.

What does all this mean for today? That we can let the hateful and hurtful comments from strangers and friends, from our own self-critical and self-shaming thoughts, and from the enemy himself, be covered by the love and gospel-work of Jesus, which was demonstrated for us on the cross. And when the voices of critics, of hate, of accusation come, we can take cover under the strong and steady love, advocacy, and justification of God. Those accusations hold no weight or power any longer—our bill has been paid, and because of Jesus, God sees us as righteous. No one can change that, and no voice can speak over the voice of our God when over us He declares: "No longer condemned." What a relief.

This also means that we can be sure that God loves us enough to not leave us as we are. He's ever growing us, ever pursuing us, that we might be truly transformed by His Love, as a display of His splendor (Isa. 61).

What might happen if we actually believed we didn't have to work to remove all our stains, but trusted that no matter how we feel, we are still uncondemned and beloved? What if we believed that the gospel actually did what God said it did? That it didn't leave some part of our sin uncovered or unpaid? The freedom and the love that we would walk in, the way we could silence any voice of accusation if we really let this truth sink in, stokes the embers of hope in my heart. I've tasted and seen how good it is when that kind of love and assurance is spoken over my most self-doubting places, and I'll be forever grateful.

- What voices in your life are most critical toward you? Do you listen to the voice of God in His Word as often as you listen to them? Why or why not?

- What part of your story are you sometimes tempted to think the gospel work of Christ did not cover?

- How might your thought-life, emotional-life, and spiritual-life look different if you truly believed that, because of Christ, you were no longer condemned before God, but forever loved and accepted?

Jesus, thank You for Your gospel work on my behalf! When the voices of accusation are closing in, help me choose to trust that because of what You did on the cross, there is a better and stronger word spoken over me: I am no longer condemned! Help me walk forward in that truth today and every day.

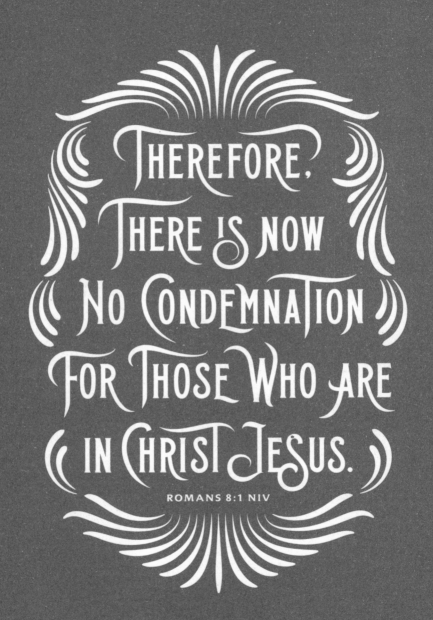

THEREFORE, THERE IS NOW NO CONDEMNATION FOR THOSE WHO ARE IN CHRIST JESUS.

ROMANS 8:1 NIV

All my longings lie open before you, Lord;
my sighing is not hidden from you.

PSALM 38:9

I don't know about you, but when my heart feels desirous of something I deeply want, I am quicker to sigh than I am to pray. This psalm is so good for my heart, because it reminds me that it is normal for us to want things.

We all know we shouldn't want things more than we want God. But that doesn't mean all our longings are wrong! Here in this psalm, the longing is for deliverance. I wonder, if you wrote a psalm today to God, what would your longings be? What do you ache for? What desires have gone unmet? This psalm tells us we don't have to hide those things or think God is mad at us for wanting them. No, it tells us to lay them open before God. To let our sighs and groanings and longings be heard instead of hidden.

I'm so grateful for the prayer book of Psalms that is smack-dab in the middle of the Bible. It makes me feel so *understood* when it comes to being human. Our desires are no surprise to God. He can handle our wants and wishes. His love meets us in those places and His ears perk up to hear our requests.

If you are in a place of crying out to God for something you've deeply desired for a long time, and feeling like He may not be hearing you, I'm sorry. Know that you are not alone. I've been there too. Keep crying out to Him. He can handle anything you need to say. He's listening, and He loves you, and this suffering and longing you have will not last forever. I am so grateful for a Love that overcomes death, for a Light that overcomes dark, and for a Lord that does not want our sighs hidden from Him. Aren't you?

- Make a list of some unmet desires you have. How do you usually handle the ache that comes with these desires?

- Why do you sometimes forget that God wants you to lay your longings out before Him?

- Although we all have certain desires or dreams that go unfulfilled today, sometimes it helps to remember the ways God has met other longings in the past. What desires or needs in your life have been met by God? How can the memory of these things help you keep coming to Him today instead of staying hidden?

God, instead of hiding all my sighs in the dark, I bring them into Your light. Help me remain in a posture of openness before You, and help me trust that You want me to keep coming to You with my longings.

For we are God's workmanship, created in Christ Jesus to do
good works, which God prepared in advance for us to do.

EPHESIANS 2:10

Do you ever wonder, "Why on earth am I here?" At some point,
I think we all feel that way. I have loved this verse for a long time
because it's been a reminder to me over and over again that I am
God's "workmanship." He made each of us on purpose and for a
purpose. I held onto this verse many days throughout my college
years. I'd get stressed out about what to declare as my major, and
then I would center in on this verse. It brought me such comfort to
know that wherever I was and whatever I was doing, I was created to
do good works, reflecting the love and light of Christ.

I ended up studying English and getting a master's degree in
education. I taught for two years and loved it, and then quit to join
my husband's band. I had no idea I'd end up doing music, writing my
own songs, or being on the career path that I'm on, but all along the
way, I've been reminded by this verse that each of us are specifically
and uniquely created and gifted to do good works, that God prepared
ahead of time for us!

A lot of times, this verse has played out in smaller ways for me.
I'd look back on my day and remember how I gave a stranger a compliment or held the door open for someone at the store with their
hands full, and I'd think, "God prepared those good works for me to
do!" I may not know exactly what those good works are all the time,
but this promise from Ephesians reminds me that God has a plan for
my life and for yours.

If you feel aimless or purposeless, take heart. God has a purpose
for you, and you don't have to understand the whole picture of how it
will all play out. God created and crafted each of us with special care

to reflect His goodness and love and peace in the world. To me this verse feels like an invitation to being fully alive and expectant for the ways God will call us to serve and love others! What if we leaned in and listened? What if we said "yes"?

- When you read that you are "God's workmanship," what is your response?

- Can you think of specific gifts that God has given you to reflect His goodness and love to the world? If not, ask God to silence every voice but His and show you some of the ways He has created you to do this.

- How might God be asking you to use the gifts He's given you in this season?

- Do you ever feel purposeless or aimless, and if so, how do you typically respond to those feelings? How does this verse speak to those feelings?

Father, thank You that I am Your workmanship, created on purpose and for a purpose. Help me to believe that You have gifted me specifically to reflect Your love and light into the world around me. On the days I feel aimless and lost, point me back to this promise and help me keep my eyes on You as I do the good works that You have prepared for me to do!

**Praise be to the Lord, to God our Savior,
who daily bears our burdens.**

PSALM 68:19

Anyone else have burdens that they are carrying around today? Maybe it's financial—some bill that needs to be paid, or spiritual—some lie from the enemy that needs to be fought. Or perhaps it's emotional—some deep pain that needs to be brought to light and tended to, or physical—some ailment that needs healing and care.

I don't know what yours looks like, but *so* many days, I carry around heavy burdens. Lately, for me, it's been the burden of fear left in the wake of an EF4 tornado that I told you about earlier in Day 81—the one that tore through our neighborhood last year. I'll never forget waking up in the middle of the night to our whole house shaking. My husband was out of town and I rushed the kids down to the basement. I've never been more scared in my life. Ever since that night, whenever there is so little as a thunderstorm, my heart begins to race and my neck and shoulders get tense. I have to breathe deep and hold onto truth to get my body and my mind to calm down. This is one of those verses I have been clinging to as the Tennessee spring storms have kicked up again. It reminds me that I can come with every wave of fear and lay it down at His feet.

So thankful for this beautiful reminder from Psalm 68:19, that God stands ready to bear every burden we place upon ourselves and every burden someone else has placed upon us too. Are you worn out from lugging around the weight of all your sorrow, struggles, and fear? What if we tried letting them go and laying them down upon our loving Father who "daily bears our burdens"? What if we really believed He wants us to offload every single burden, every single day into His strong and capable arms?

- What specific burdens are you carrying right now?
- What comfort does it bring to you to meditate on this verse in light of those burdens you're carrying?
- What keeps you from entrusting the burdens you carry to the care of Jesus?

Father, You know the burden I carry today unlike any other person could possibly know it. Please help me believe that You stand ready to receive it. Help me lay it down and give me the strength to leave it in Your hands.

He will swallow up death forever. The Sovereign
LORD will wipe away the tears from all faces.

ISAIAH 25:8A

When we think of Jesus, so often, we spend time looking back at what He did when He first came. How He wrapped Himself in flesh to enter our broken world so that He could be broken for us, and we could be made whole. How He grew up and lived sinlessly. How He died in our place, to secure us a bright future forever. How He was resurrected to prove He has the power to defeat death.

It is a beautiful story to remember and to tell over and over again, of course, but recently I've been learning to look in a new direction. Not just *back* at when Jesus came to this weary world, but *forward*, as we wait for Him to come again. There will be a day when He will make everything new, when He will wipe away the tears from all faces, and on days when I look at the world and see so much sorrow and suffering and injustice, my heart longs for Him to return. And this is the beauty of what we celebrate when we think about Jesus. We can know that whatever sorrow we are facing isn't the end of the story, because He will come again to make all things right. We can know that He didn't just come once, He will come *finally* and *forever*, and all those promises He's made us in His Word about resurrection life really will come to fruition.

I came across this statement the other day and just loved it: "'Come, Lord Jesus,' is not a cry of desperation, but an assured shout of cosmic hope."[5] Christ has come, and He will come again! Grateful for this truth and this hope today. Come, Lord Jesus!

- When you think of Jesus, what part of His life or ministry comes to mind first? Why?

- What might change in your life if you not only looked back at what Jesus has done for you, but also looked forward at what He's coming to do?

- How might your perspective change if you prayed "Come, Lord Jesus" over every area of strife or struggle in your life? Make a list of hard situations or circumstances in which you long to see the redeeming work of Christ at hand, and pray "Come, Lord Jesus" over each one.

Jesus, thank You for what You came to do for me—and thank You also for all You will do when You come again! Please help me look forward to that day, and give me faith and hope to live in light of it all of my days. Remind me to pray "Come, Lord Jesus," as an "assured shout of cosmic hope" in the face of the brokenness in my own heart and in the world around me.

Show me the right path, O LORD; point out the road for me to follow. Lead me by your truth and teach me, for you are the God who saves me. All day long I put my hope in you.

PSALM 25:4–5 NLT

Have you ever seen the movie *Up*? There are multiple scenes where dogs are talking, and in the middle of their conversation, they will stop mid-sentence and jerk their heads in the same direction, as suddenly one of them shouts, "SQUIRREL!" I don't know about you, but this is how I feel a lot of days!

There is so much to get done. There are so many people to love and serve, and there are so many good things I could do with my moments and my days. Yet, in the bustle of it all and in the seemingly endless number of things that need squaring away, this verse centers me. It reminds me that I can ask God to guide my steps and my moments, and I've found that when I do that, there is a letting go, a rest, and a calmness that comes over me. I'm suddenly anchored in His love and His truth, listening to how He might direct me, even with a *full* and busy day on my hands.

In fact, as I was writing this very paragraph, I was simultaneously trying to decide on how to best travel with my kids for an upcoming show, and I had to remind myself that instead of circling round and round the decision in my head, which is what I usually do, I had the option to bring it to God, who guides me, who leads me, who saves me. And you know what? He did all those things. He helped me see "the road for me to follow." He always does, no matter what decision we face or squirrel we chase. Thankful for a trustworthy guide and friend in the Lord today.

- Why do you think we sometimes forget to invite God to guide our steps and our schedules?

- How might the next month look different if you allowed Him to do that?

- In what situation do you need direction today? Where might you need God to "point out the road for [you] to follow"?

God, You know the road before me, even if I cannot see it. You know which way I should go, and You promise to point it out if I invite You to do so. I come to You today, trusting this promise, and asking You for direction. Give me eyes to see and ears to hear You as You guide me down the right path.

And being in anguish, he prayed more earnestly . . .

LUKE 22:44

It's not like the world hasn't gone through its fair share of suffering. Surely, over the course of human history, it has. But when the Covid-19 pandemic descended on the world back in 2020, it's like a fresh outpouring of suffering covered the whole globe. And that suffering took so many different forms. People lost their lives to the virus. Others lost their jobs. Others lost friends. Some people lost their homes. Plenty of us felt like we were losing our sanity. I remember being so disoriented and confused; but one thing that helped my perspective as the days turned into weeks and months and years, was that our Savior has suffered too.

This verse is about Jesus in the Garden of Gethsemane the night He was betrayed. He knows what is to come, knows that His own blood will be shed for the saving of many, and begs God to find another way. He's sweating blood. He's in anguish. And it's here in this place we see Jesus pray all the more earnestly. It's here in this place Jesus says, "and yet, not my will, but yours be done" (Luke 22:42).

And with that humble and honest obedience, Jesus makes a way through every crisis, through every anguish, through every chaotic season the human race would ever face. He descends into death, into a grave, into hell itself. What does that mean? It means that in terms of pain, *there is no place He has not been*. There is no pain He cannot overcome. There is no darkness His light won't undo.

This truth brought me great comfort when the pandemic was just in its beginning stages, and it still gives me great comfort today when I face sorrow of any kind. It helps me remember that we can earnestly pray to a God who is not far from the suffering. We can earnestly pray to a God who has made a way through the grave to ensure that our suffering really will come to an end one day. Today

I bring my heavy heart to the foot of the cross, knowing that Jesus knows what anguish feels like, and that the anguish you and I face today is not the final act of God's story for us.

- What was the start of the pandemic like for you? What did you lose? How did you feel?

- What places of anguish exist in your life today? What's your typical reaction to them?

- This verse shows us that the more Jesus' anguish deepened, the deeper He went into prayer. Is this what anguish and prayer look like in your life? Why or why not?

- How does it change things to know that there's no place of pain Jesus hasn't been?

Father, You know the anguish I have experienced. The deeper the pain goes, help me lean all the more into You, for You know exactly what anguish feels like. Help me, in this moment, to trust Your will and Your ways. Give me the strength to continue coming to You, no matter how heavy my heart is.

When I said, "My foot is slipping," your unfailing
love, LORD, supported me. When anxiety was great
within me, your consolation brought me joy.

PSALM 94:18-19

When I look back over my life, there have been so many desperate moments of me crying out, "Lord! My foot is slipping!" Have I used these exact words? Nope. But I know that feeling when the weight of everything I am facing feels like it's going to crush me. I have known anxiety that feels like the weight of an elephant on my chest, sometimes for no reason at all. If you have heavy days like this too, you probably know exactly what I mean.

These are the moments we tend to cry out for help . . . the desperate moments. *Lord, if You don't show up, I'm not gonna make it through this breath . . . this season . . . this trial.* It's so helpful to look back at these times in our lives because, although they are dark, we get the chance to truly know God's consolation. The definition of *consolation* is, "The comfort received by a person after a loss or disappointment."[6] And I can honestly say I've gotten to experience this kind of comfort in some of my most desperate moments.

If you feel like your foot is slipping, or if anxiety is great within you today, my prayer is that you'll rest awhile in His love and know the comfort of the One who has been to hell and back for you. I'm so grateful that we can receive comfort from a God who knows what it is to lose something, a God who knows we would all face loss and disappointment and death, and a God who gave up everything so that loss and disappointment and even death would not lay final claim to us.

- In what way is your foot slipping today?

- What do you typically use to "support" yourself when you feel this way? Has it proven sturdy enough for you?

- In what ways is God's love and consolation a better support for your desperate moments?

- What would resting awhile in God's love look like for you this week?

🔥 Lord, my foot is slipping! Please show up. I believe Your love is strong enough to support me, and I ask for Your consolation in this moment. Hold me up, and help me lean into the support You always offer to me.

The Word became flesh and made his dwelling among us. We have seen his glory, the glory of the one and only Son, who came from the Father, full of grace and truth.

JOHN 1:14

"Full of grace and truth." Isn't it amazing that Jesus is both? I was recently studying the book of John, and in the course of the journey, I realized that Jesus really does show us a balance of these throughout His ministry. He's not afraid to tell people the hard truth sometimes. He has a way of holding out reality in front of people instead of letting them stay in deception. Yet, as we trace His steps, we also see that He's not afraid to extend grace, either. He's full of compassion and help for the lowly! I came across a book that explained the best translation of the word *grace* in this verse: "When the one from whom I have a right to expect nothing gives me everything."[7]

Don't you love that? I do! I am undone with the fact that when we face the truth of who we really are with all of our shortcomings, Jesus holds out grace to us, going to the cross on our behalf for all those shortcomings, pouring His light and love and life out for us, even when we don't deserve it. That's how truth and grace work together—one reveals our actual state of affairs before God, and the other one fixes that sad state of affairs, covering it with love!

This is good news. This is the gospel. I don't know about you, but that makes me want to shout out along with John, "We have seen his glory! The glory of the one and only Son!"

- When you think of Jesus, does His character lean more toward "truth" or "grace" in your mind? Why?

- Why is it important that Jesus is full of both truth and grace?

- How have you seen these two qualities of Jesus work together for good in your life?

Jesus, thank You for being full of both grace and truth, and thank You for drawing near to the world instead of abandoning it. Thank You for drawing near to ME, even today.

Do you not know?
Have you not heard?
The LORD is the everlasting God,
the Creator of the ends of the earth.
He will not grow tired or weary,
and his understanding no one can fathom.
He gives strength to the weary and
increases the power of the weak.
Even youths grow tired and weary,
and young men stumble and fall;
but those who hope in the LORD
will renew their strength.
They will soar on wings like eagles;
they will run and not grow weary,
they will walk and not be faint.

ISAIAH 40:28–31

It's been 100 days of you and me sitting in God's promises and asking Him to help us believe that they are true! What a journey it's been, and what a kind and faithful God we have encountered. He doesn't grow tired or weary of having to remind His forgetful children of His faithful, steady, wonderfully strong love for us. God's love doesn't waver, even though we do. God's love doesn't run out or dry up or pack up and leave. God doesn't shake His head at us when we forget or mess up; He meets us in our messes, shines light into our darkness, leaves the ninety-nine to come find us, puts us on His shoulders and carries us back home. We can't fathom His patience or His understanding. He operates in upside-down and backward ways, using our weakness and brokenness to reveal His strength and power to heal even the most broken places in our hearts. Using our "not enough" to showcase His "more than enough." Using death itself, the loss of His own Son, to bring about life everlasting.

I hope that this book will be one you treasure for years to come. I hope that maybe it's helped you bury some treasure deep within your heart as you've joined me in memorizing Scripture. I hope that on those nights when the lies are loud and the pain feels impossible to bear, that you'll recall some of the promises that we've held onto together, and hold on for dear life. I hope you'll begin to speak the light from God's Word into the darkest corners of your heart and into this weary world. I hope that the enemy will be thwarted over and over again as he tries to get you to believe anything but the truth that God's love can carry you through everything. I hope that these verses fill your heart with anticipation, spill out of your mouth as you pray and talk with friends and family, and continue to remind you that you can overcome anything you'll ever face when you're in the hands of a Love who has overcome the grave. I hope that spending one hundred days of gazing at Him and His promises has filled you with your own fighting words:

Truth to hold up like a flashlight in the darkest nights of your soul.

Truth to anchor you in Love when the shame storms blow in.

Truth to lift your eyes to the hills when you are walking through the valley of the shadow of death.

Truth to set you free and fill your soul with hope even in your most hopeless places.

Truth that breaks the chains and sets you free to be exactly who God made you to be.

Finally, I hope and pray that together, you and I will press on. Our work is to remember, and to keep kicking back at the shadows with the light. Our verse to end this devotional tells us that those who hope in the Lord will renew their strength. So let's keep hoping. Let's keep holding on to the truth and seeing our strength renewed. Let's keep using our fighting words. Let's keep speaking them into the darkness, and watch the light of the truth shine bright like a beacon that guides us back home into the arms of Love. Let's remember that the days of darkness are numbered and that there is a moment fast approaching when the darkness will fully and finally lose to the Light.

I will fight the lies with the truth
Keep my eyes fixed on You
I will sing the truth into the dark
I will use my fighting words.

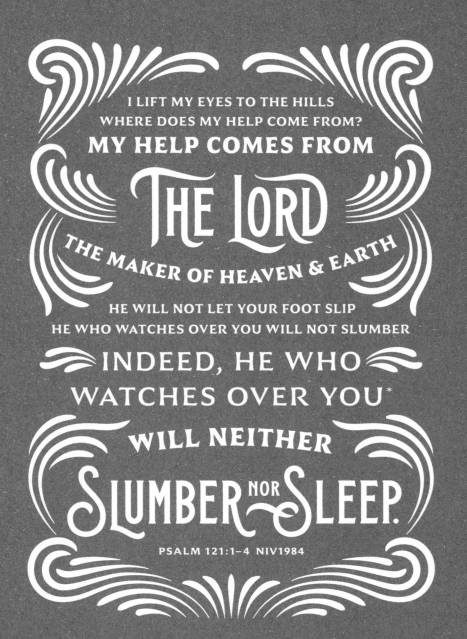

I LIFT MY EYES TO THE HILLS
WHERE DOES MY HELP COME FROM?
MY HELP COMES FROM

THE LORD

THE MAKER OF HEAVEN & EARTH

HE WILL NOT LET YOUR FOOT SLIP
HE WHO WATCHES OVER YOU WILL NOT SLUMBER

INDEED, HE WHO
WATCHES OVER YOU*
WILL NEITHER

SLUMBER NOR SLEEP.

PSALM 121:1–4 NIV1984

*lit., Israel

I lift my eyes to the hills—where does my help come
from? My help comes from the LORD, the Maker of
heaven and earth. He will not let your foot slip—he who
watches over you will not slumber; indeed, he who
watches over Israel will neither slumber nor sleep.

PSALM 121:1–4 NIV1984

I've been singing this verse to comfort my heart in times of trouble
for years now. When the melody first came to me, I was volunteering
to sing at a camp in Colorado, with an organization that I love called
Young Life. (If you've already read through the last 100 days, you probably already know how much I love this organization and how many
memories are dear to me because of it!) We were a new family of five,
our precious baby boy was nine months old, and we were all serving
together for two weeks. We have volunteered countless summers at
Young Life camps, and I have always loved connecting with kids from
all over the country; but with our three kiddos in tow, I felt completely
pulled in every direction, trying to manage all of our responsibilities
with our musical roles at the camp, meeting and connecting with hundreds of campers each week, while also trying to spend quality time
with our kids—not to mention nursing a baby. I was stretched thin.

Have you ever been in those "thin" places—the ones where you
feel pulled between so many things, you're failing to do any one thing
well? This was me. I felt like a terrible mom, a distracted conversation-
alist with high school kids, and a forgetful musician who kept missing
lyrics and playing wrong chords. I had rushed back to our room to
pump so the babysitter could feed our boy during the concert later
that night, and I found myself crying while doing so. I was exhausted,
and I felt like a failure. It was in this very low moment that I happened
to glance out the window. Surrounding the camp were absolutely

beautiful mountains, summer-green with snow-capped tops. They stretched up into the bluebird sky, and all of the sudden this beautiful verse came to mind. I started to sing a melody to these words that immediately began to slow my tears and lower my heart rate:

"I lift my eyes to the hills—where does my help come from?"

I was in an emotional valley, feeling keenly aware of my "not enough," but as I stared at those beautiful mountains, I was reminded of who made them, of who made me. I was also reminded of who was with me, even in the places where I felt stretched thin, too weak for the journey ahead. I certainly felt like I had some mountains to scale in my life during that season. I was managing a career, the transition to three kids, as well as walking through some heartache with dear friends of ours, but as I lifted my eyes to the literal hills around me that afternoon, God was so kind to remind me that I don't ever have to walk through valleys or climb mountains alone.

There is a Companion who watches over us, a tender Shepherd who guides, leads, carries, and loves us through every low place and every difficult climb. God is an incredible caregiver, and His love never slumbers or sleeps. We may get exhausted. We may get stretched thin. But He never grows too tired or too weary to take care of His children. What a gift!

This truth means that we can rest, knowing we are held in the everlasting arms of the One who made us and knows us best. His arms can hold all the things we feel responsible to carry. His arms can catch all the balls we drop and carry all the burdens that are simply too heavy for us along the way. He knows the path and can guide us upward. He's so near, even in the depths of the deepest valleys. When the climb is steep and feels scary, He watches over us and won't let our feet slip. God, who made the mountains, knows the way up from the valley. He knows the way down too, and this is one of the most powerful things I have experienced in my life. In EVERY valley I've ever walked through, every hollowed-out, grieving, dark, and lonely place, I've encountered the kindness and love of God leading me through the darkness of a lowly valley and then back up again toward the light.

Sometimes it takes being in a valley for me to see the mountains of grace that surround. Sometimes it takes coming to the end of my rope, to the end of my resources, to the end of myself, to get to the beginning of God's endless love and strength. Sometimes it takes my head bent low with exhaustion, fear, or grief to know the comfort of the hand of God, gently lifting my chin so I can behold the power of the gospel even in my deepest losses, darkest nights, and steepest climbs. *Oh God, help me remember, especially on the valley days when I feel overwhelmed by the journey ahead of me, to lift my eyes to the hills and remember where my help comes from.*

- What valleys are you walking through, or what metaphorical mountains (challenges or troubles) are you facing right now?

- I SO often forget that I can carry my burdens and worries and failures to God. Is it easy or hard for you to ask for help when you feel stretched thin? Why?

- Can you think of a time when you felt that your foot was slipping and you were met by the stable hands of God? If so, write it down to remind yourself of the help God has given you in the past. If not, ask God to come now and steady your steps.

Oh God, steady companion, when I feel overwhelmed and weary, remind me to be quick to lift my eyes to the hills and remember that You are my kind and constant Keeper. Oh Maker of mountains and stars, of hills and valleys, help me remember the whole world was made by Your Word and is held in Your hands. When I am in the valley places, give me the vision to see Your unshakable love supporting me. Thank You for walking beside me, and for always being there to catch me with arms of mercy and grace when it feels like my feet are about to slip. Thank You that I know where my help comes from. Help me rest as I remember that Your love never slumbers or sleeps.

If you'd like to sing this psalm with me, it's written into the song called "I Lift My Eyes" on my album, *All of My Days.*

DAY
102

Be kind to one another, tenderhearted, forgiving
one another, as God in Christ forgave you.

EPHESIANS 4:32 ESV

The other day my kids were all arguing about something silly. Do any other parents out there feel like referees in their own homes some days?! Their tones with each other were harsh and angry, and they all needed to take some space to calm their little bodies down. After a full family time-out, I made them all sit in a circle holding hands. They don't love this at first, but usually it ends up making them laugh, and then I had them sing this verse with me.

This precious verse is an atmosphere-changer in our home. It points us back to the Author of love and forgiveness, and reminds us that we can be kind and tenderhearted because God is kind and tenderhearted toward us. It's amazing what happens, for both me and my kids, when we simply remember we're loved and forgiven. It expands our hearts to be able to love and forgive in ways we might never be able to on our own. It is such a gentle reminder to be gentle with others—and with ourselves!—because God is gentle with us.

This is also the verse I sing over myself when I notice my heart beating fast in anger or frustration with my kids or even random people on the internet. It reminds me that I get to live from a place of belonging, being fully known AND fully loved. When I remember that I am loved despite all my shortcomings and all my mistakes, something shifts in my heart. I remember to give mercy and grace. I remember to forgive. I remember that no matter who I'm frustrated with—whether it be my own child, the slow car in front of me in traffic, or a stranger online—they are made in the image of God and they are all fighting their own battles. Empathy floods in, and as Love takes anger's hand, I am reminded to take a deep breath and remember that every beating human heart is precious to God. The anger and frustration pass, and I'm able to move forward in peace. Forgiving others always does this for my heart. It helps me both acknowledge the pain or frustration, AND let it go so it doesn't continue to harm me or cause my body stress and anxiety.

I love the invitation this verse gives to me and to my kids, over and over again: Remember love, and then walk in love. What a beautiful way to live!

- Sometimes it helps me to reflect on how I might have been unkind to myself or to others because I can identify places in which I may not be walking in love. Take a moment to reflect on this for yourself and write down what comes to mind.

- I hope these next questions help you practice walking in forgiveness today. I know I certainly always need practice! Especially when I want to forgive someone else, this is never a one-time-deal for me. I usually end up having to choose forgiveness over and over again. Please remember as you answer these questions that when we ask for forgiveness, God is so faithful to always give it in abundance.

  · Is there anything you need forgiveness for? Ask for it now.

  · Is there anyone in your life you'd like to speak forgiveness over? They might not have said they are sorry or even acknowledged that they have hurt you, but I do think this verse gives us an invitation to both acknowledge the hurt we have and to let go of it in the presence of God's love so it doesn't have as much power over us. (Keep in mind that forgiveness does not mean continuing in unsafe or unhealthy relationship patterns.)

· Is there anyone you'd like to ask forgiveness from? Take a moment and pray about asking for it. We can't always guarantee other's will give us forgiveness, but my goodness, it's such a beautiful practice to walk out with each other. Ask God to give you courage to own your mistakes and say you're sorry. I have found a LOT of freedom in doing this for my soul, and I pray you will too!

— I love the phrase "tender-hearted." Sometimes my heart feels more hardened like stone rather than tender. Take a moment now to ask God to show you any places in your heart that need tenderness. Write out the hard-as-stone places and pray this verse over each one.

— How could you walk in more tenderness and kindness today? Not only with others, but with yourself?

Thank You, God, for leading me in a kind and tenderhearted way. Thank You for the forgiveness You so freely offer to me. May I be a person marked by kindness, a tender heart, and a deep and wide forgiveness that brings healing and wholeness to myself, my family, and my community.

DAY
103

So then, just as you received Christ Jesus as Lord,
continue to live your lives in him, rooted and built
up in him, strengthened in the faith as you were
taught, and overflowing with thankfulness."

COLOSSIANS 2:6-7

Did you know that a Tulip Poplar's roots go as deep as the branches go high? That is wild to me! We have two of these massive and magical trees in our backyard, and I'm grateful for the shade they provide in the summer, for the golden color every fall, and for the bright orange and lime green flowers they drop like presents in our yard each spring. When I think about this verse, I think about how I want to be like the Tulip Poplars in our backyard, with roots that run as deep as possible into the love of God.

So often, though, it feels like my roots get a little mixed up. Does this ever happen to you? My roots either don't run deep enough, or they sink down deep into something other than the love of God. Often I'll have roots that run into my own strength, or that try to find security and be built up in my work or my role as a mom, a friend, or a wife. Can you imagine if this verse gave us the opposite instruction? "Just as you received Christ Jesus as Lord, continue to live your lives in him, rooted and built up . . ."

"in your own strength?!"

Or, *"in how well your work is going?!"*

Or *"in how many likes you get on some social media post?!"*

When I send my roots to find a firm foundation in these lesser things, I end up the opposite of grateful. Instead of "overflowing with thankfulness," I am usually overflowing with self-focus, worry, and anxiety—and NO wonder! We are not meant to bear the weight of our lives and the work and the pain and the ache of being a human alone. I'm SO grateful for this kind instruction to send our roots down into the stable, sure, and strong love of God. This means we don't have to muster up love or strength on our own; instead, we get to go straight to the source of all love and take all that we need.

My prayer is that as I send my roots deep into the nourishment of God's grace, into the current of living water, that my life will produce color and shade and flowers for all those around me. I pray this for my children as well, and for you. May we establish ourselves in the sturdy love of God, and then live with hearts and lives overflowing with that same source of all life and light, abounding with thanksgiving! Or, as Eugene Peterson would put it:

> My counsel for you is simple and straightforward: Just go ahead with what you've been given. You received Christ Jesus, the Master; now live him. You're deeply rooted in him. You're well constructed upon him. You know your way around the faith. Now do what you've been taught. School's out; quit studying the subject and start *living* it! And let your living spill over into thanksgiving. (Col. 2:6–7 MSG)

- What places or people or things do you tend to send your roots into as you look for a firm foundation?
- Do you find these places sufficient for grounding your spirit and soul? What do they lack?
- What might it look like for you to send your roots into the love of God?
- What do you hope overflows from your life into the people around you?

Oh God, thank You for being a sure and sturdy place to send down my roots when I need nourishment and sustaining grace. Help me see the lesser places I've tried to find a firm foundation—the places that always crumble beneath my feet—and then give me the strength to redirect my roots back to You. You are a good God who never runs out of mercy and love. I pray You'll make me like the Tulip Poplar, growing both deep and high into Your great love.

DAY
104

He has made everything beautiful in its time. He also set
eternity in the human heart: yet no one can fathom what
God has done from beginning to end. I know that there is
nothing better for the people than to be happy and to do
good while they live. That each of them may eat and drink.
And find satisfaction in all their toil—this is the gift of God.

ECCLESIASTES 3:11–13

This verse has been a deep encouragement to me during this
season of life that feels so divided on so many levels. It's good for me
to remember that a day is coming, where everything will be set right,
made beautiful again. If eternity is set in the human heart, then it
makes sense that we all long for this . . . for all to be well.

The problem is, I think we all have different ideas of what "all
being well in eternity" might look like, and of how to get there,
and so . . . we fight. I watch with deep sadness on social media as
image-bearing brothers and sisters in Christ use the comments
section to type hate and judgment out toward other image-bearers.
I wonder how such dissonance and hostility can ever be restored
into something harmonious and peaceful. It feels like we can do
better than this.

I love that this verse affirms that no one can totally fathom what
God has done from beginning to end. It gives me deep comfort in this
chaotic, broken world, that there is no way to fathom all the ways
God is moving with love and healing in our midst. It reminds me there
is a massive element of following Jesus that requires getting com-
fortable with mystery, with not fully knowing everything. This is both
humbling and such a gift on the days when my human brain can't
comprehend how God will restore all things one day.

I love how this verse in Ecclesiastes gives a nod to this struggle and yet also simultaneously gives some tangible ways to move forward through the struggle and the mystery. While we long for that future day when every tear will be wiped away, there's this solid dose of wisdom from this passage: there's nothing better than doing good, being happy, and finding satisfaction in all of our work. It feels so simple, AND so hard. Find satisfaction in all our work? Even in the moments it feels like "toil"? Some days feel impossible, but I wonder if we focused on the fact that we have a purpose on this earth—to love big and do good—if it would change our perspectives at work?

This feels like such a friendly reminder to myself to aim to do a little good in the world today . . . say a kind word, pay for someone's meal, donate to a cause I love, pick up some trash, give a compliment, to do my work with integrity and excellence, to lend a helping hand, or read a book that helps me understand someone else's perspective. It also gently reminds us that the work we do, whatever it is, can be a gift to us and to others, especially when we lead with gratitude and joy.

I pray that I'll be marked by a hope that one day everything will be made beautiful, and until that day comes, I pray to be the kind of person who does a lot of good, laughs loud, and works hard all my days.

- What place of division and chaos do you especially long for eternity—for the love of God—to come heal and redeem and restore? Take a moment to bring these longings in prayer before the Lord.

- How might you be able to do good today? This week? This year? Ponder and write down some ways you could do that at work and at home.

- Gratitude often helps me to find satisfaction in whatever it is I am doing, so take a moment to write out different things you are grateful for in your work life and in your home life.

Thank You, God, that even in the midst of a broken and chaotic world, You are moving. When I feel overwhelmed with the division and chaos around me, may I remember that You are a bridge builder, that You make everything beautiful in its time, and that even on the days I can't imagine how, You *will* restore all things one day. Help me to bear witness to this beautiful truth by doing good wherever I am, and by finding satisfaction in You and in all the work You have given me to do while I'm here—whether in my home, my community, or my city. May I live a life that finds goodness and joy in the ordinary moments and tasks.

My heart, O God, is steadfast; I will sing
and make music with all my soul.
Awake, harp and lyre! I will awaken the dawn.
I will praise you, LORD, among the nations;
I will sing of you among the peoples.
For great is your love, higher than the heavens;
your faithfulness reaches to the skies.
Be exalted, O God, above the heavens;
let your glory be over all the earth.
Save us and help us with your right hand,
that those you love may be delivered.

PSALM 108:1-6

I love these verses from Psalm 108. It was actually the first passage of Scripture that made me want to sing! I was in high school when I started humming a melody to help me carry these beautiful words in my heart.

"My heart is steadfast, Oh God, I will sing
and make music with all my soul."

I had no idea that I was going to become a musician when I was a freshman in high school. I mainly remember just wanting to make the soccer team and hang out with my friends. But I also wanted to sing this because my heart didn't feel steadfast at the time. I knew enough about God to know that He loved me and had good plans for me, but my heart felt scattered and distracted (as the hearts of many freshman high school girls probably feel!). Looking back now, I can see that there must have been something in me that knew I'd need to hold onto these words.

Truthfully, I didn't really trust that God's love would be enough for me in that time of my life, so I looked elsewhere. I fell in love with a senior boy at my high school, and he fell in love with me. It felt like a dream at that age—like I was living a Taylor Swift song that had a happy ending—but I let this boy quickly become the sole source of my worth. He was my safe place in the world, and while it truly was a sweet and very innocent relationship, it completely replaced my awareness of my need and longing for a love that reaches higher than the heavens.

The boy left for college. We dated long distance for two years, and ultimately, he broke it off. My identity and worth were shattered right alongside my heart.

I don't think that my high school self knew it, but I was desperately searching for identity and love. Aren't we all? We are hardwired for it. I love that I started singing these verses from Psalm 108 all those years ago. They whispered about a love that never lets me go, a love that came before me and goes behind me. I wanted to drink deeply of that kind of love. Singing this psalm reminded my distrusting and forgetful heart that there is a love that reaches to the heavens. I sang it often in the wake of my heart breaking, asking the Lord to save me with His right hand, to heal me, and to remind me that there is a steadfast LOVE that will forever be faithful and will never let me go. I didn't know it fully then, but I surely know it now: *God doesn't change His mind about loving us.* I once heard my pastor say, "There's nothing you could do that would make God love you more than He already does, and there's nothing you could do to make God love you less than He already does." What a comfort!

You may be searching for your worth and your identity like I was. You may have forgotten, like I sometimes do, that you are dearly loved by the God who made you. My prayer is that this verse reminds you that you're surrounded by the sturdy, immovable, faithful love of God, and *nothing* will ever change that. Really coming to trust that this is true has made my heart want to sing to all the peoples and all the nations about a God who holds onto us, even when we let go. There is a God whose love for us reaches to the skies, and when we can settle into that love and trust that it is NEVER going anywhere and that God will be able to love us better than any human will ever be able to love us, it changes everything. When we are grounded in a love that reaches to the skies, we can come into every relationship, not searching for our worth or our identity, but assured of our deep value as precious children of God. Let's hold on to that truth today, no matter what or who we encounter.

— As you read these verses, notice how God's love reaches to the heavens, but also reaches down to hold your hand. Take a moment to lift your eyes to the sky (don't look directly at the sun!). Imagine a love extending higher than you can see and then reaching all the way down to your heart. How does it make you feel to know that there is a love that BIG for you?

— Have you ever tried to find your worth in something other than God's love, like I did? If so, how is that working for you? How would it change your life if you began to truly find your worth and identity in God's unfailing love for you?

— Write a few lines of gratitude for this faithful, unwavering love of God. Maybe even write your own song! You don't have to sing it. But maybe do! :) What would it look like to "sing" of God's love, even if you don't actually sing about it? Why do you think God invites us to do this? Why do you think it might be good for us to do this?

Oh God, Your loving kindness reaches to the heavens. Would You lift my eyes to the heavens above—with clouds and sun during the days and littered with stars at night—to remind my forgetful heart that Your love for me stretches even beyond the sky? Would You steady my shaky heart with Your sturdy hand, and help me sing of Your faithfulness all the days of my life? Thank You for being a God that anchors my identity and always stays true to me, no matter what.

If you'd like to sing this psalm with me, it's written into
the song called "My Heart Is Steadfast" on my album, *All of My Days*.

"For the bread of God is he who comes down
from heaven and gives life to the world."

"Sir," they said, "from now on give us this bread."

Then Jesus declared, "I am the bread of life. He
who comes to me will never go hungry, and he
who believes in me will never be thirsty."

JOHN 6:33–35

We had some family friends over for dinner and one of them, Matt, who is an incredible cook, had spent the day making his first batch of sourdough bread. He brought it to share, fresh out of the oven, and we delighted in the crunch followed by a shower of crumbs as we broke the loaf into smaller pieces to share. It was delicious—and this is one of the reasons why I love this passage from John. I mean, who doesn't love bread?

For context, there is a group of people by a lake asking Jesus a boatload of questions. They had just asked Him for a miraculous sign to help them believe that God really did send Him to be the Messiah. They remind Jesus of how God provided for the Israelites with manna in the desert, and then Jesus responds with verse 33:

"For the bread of God is he who comes down
from heaven and gives life to the world."

Now, I like to imagine that these people had been at the lake all day and that they were hungry. No theological merit to that statement at all, but I'm always hungry at the lake. (Anyone else with me here? If it was possible to print a cry-laughing emoji, I'd put one here.) I make

254

this point because I relate so much to the response of the people listening to Jesus talk about a bread that gives LIFE to the world.

"Sir, from now on give us this bread."

I love these people. First of all, they were lake-hungry and just wanted something to eat. Second, Jesus is saying that this bread actually gives LIFE. This resonates with me in so many ways, so I feel like I'd be in the chorus of asking Jesus to give me THAT bread . . . the LIFE bread from now on.

I love that they didn't realize they were talking with the Bread of Life. They didn't know that they were listening to the voice who first called all things into creation. They wanted the bread that they had seen or heard of before, the manna that fell from heaven, but they had the source of all LIFE sitting right next to them there at the lake. They wanted a little miracle manna snack, and they had the author of all miracles and all good things in their midst. This feels so familiar to me. So often I'll be asking for the answer, for the problem to go away, for something to change and frustrated that it's not going like I want it to go, when *God* is right beside me, offering His companionship and grace and presence to me.

Don't get me wrong. I'm still a big fan of asking for what we need, for asking like kids. The Bible tells us to do that, and I've seen God move in both big ways and in small details, meeting needs when I ask for provision. But what I really don't want to miss is the actual presence of Bread that satisfies even in the desert places, that nourishes in the valleys, that soaks up our tears when we can't stop crying.

Speaking of valleys and tears, I have just clung to this verse in the wake of an awful tragedy—a school shooting—in our city of Nashville. It was the stuff of nightmares, and the losses are deep and wide. We have grieved. We are grieving. We'll never be the same, and yet, in our midst, as we have wept, as we have comforted our children who were scared to go back to school, as we have gathered to pray over families who long to hold their babies again, we have known the comfort and nearness of Jesus, the Bread of Life, who meets us and fills us up even in the grave places, reminding us that even though we grieve, death is never the end. Hope rises.

There is much work to be done to better protect our children in schools across this country, and to help provide for those who are mentally ill. We're still processing, still advocating, still longing for change, still wishing we had the precious ones we loved back. Even though our whole world in Nashville still aches, we also still live, and it is in this moving forward with a gaping hole in our hearts, that we ask: *Oh Lord, give us the Bread of Life. Show us Your light in the midst of this darkness; sustain, heal, and satisfy us with Your love and compassion.*

— What have you been asking God for lately?

— Do you feel like He is listening? Why or why not?

— What would it look like to imagine that even as you bring your heart and desires to God, that He is right in your midst?

— Take a moment to write out some memories of God bringing life to you even in desert seasons, satisfying and sustaining you with His presence, then thank Him for being your sustenance, your Bread of Life during that season and on this day as well.

God, thank You for the way You welcome my questions and longings and desires. Thank You that even as I come to You with my heart and hopes and griefs and joys, You are in my midst. Help me to remember, especially when I feel that I am lacking something, that Jesus came to give me life and that His love swallowed up death itself. May I remember to hold onto THIS bread, the Bread of Heaven who lived out love in a way that changed the world. Help me to nourish my soul with this story and share this Bread of Life with all those I encounter.

The LORD your God is in your midst,
a mighty one who will save;
he will rejoice over you with gladness;
he will quiet you by his love;
he will exult over you with loud singing.

ZEPHANIAH 3:17 ESV

When I realized that this precious promise from Zephaniah was not in the original edition of *Fighting Words*, I gasped out loud! It is one of my absolute favorite verses and grounded one of my favorite songs that I've written, "I Don't Want to Miss It." I still remember the first time I read this verse in high school. A precious older friend and teammate wrote it out on an index card and handed it to me the day of our regional soccer tournament. I was starting in the game that night for one of the first times in my high school soccer life. I was nervous, and she knew it. She handed me that little card to carry around in my pocket all day as a reminder of God's love for me. I remember immediately taking a deep breath when I read it, and then sitting in awe and wonder that the God who made the universe also SINGS over us. All these years later, I'm still carrying this truth around in my pocket. It's one of the promises that has sunk deep down to a soul level, and I'm so grateful!

This verse took on a whole new meaning to me in the past few years. Throughout a year or two of counseling, I spent time visiting some of the deepest wounds in my story. I've acknowledged them before, of course, but since I have the sort of personality that avoids pain at all costs, I've never actually spent much time there in the pits of my deepest sorrows. But as I simply allowed myself to go back to those places and breathe and grieve and weep, I encountered the breath and life and love and tenderness and empathy of God.

It's not an easy commitment to hike down into the valley of our deepest wounds, into the deepest part of the canyons of pain that life can carve out of us. Sometimes it feels like that journey might kill us. But there, in the valley, I encountered God's love. In those places where I felt the most out of control, the most sad, the most angry, the most hurt . . . I found that I was held and sung over, just like I hold and sing over my kids.

God will quiet us by His love if we'll only let Him. He's singing over us on our saddest days *and* He's singing over us when we are on our A-game and thriving in life. He's singing over us when we're lost *and* when we are found. He's singing over us when we are missing the mark *and* when we are hitting every target. He's singing over us when we feel that we look our best *and* when we know that we're at our worst. He delights over us with loud singing, *and* He quiets us with His love, like a mother sings a lullaby to calm her baby.

As I said before, when I wrote the song "I Don't Want to Miss It," I grounded it in this Scripture. My hope is that in a VERY noisy world, that somehow we can turn up the volume of the song of LOVE God sings over every beating human heart! I don't want to miss any of His beauty or any of His love. Jesus says that He comes to give us life to the full (John 10:10), and as I get older and experience more sorrow—as my eyes have been opened to more of the pain that others on this earth experience and to the pain I have carried in my own story—I'm seeing a clearer picture. I'm seeing that we have the opportunity to experience the FULLNESS of God's love, presence, peace, and power in the FULL spectrum of life. From the tops of the mountains to the depths of the valleys, from our deepest sorrows to our brightest joys, God is there . . . singing over us, the whole time.

You are held. You are loved. Whether life is full of noise or pain or joy for you right now, know that in every season, God rejoices over you—you specifically—with singing. He made you on purpose and for a purpose. He loves you, and He's with you always. I'm so grateful for this good news today, and I hope that this verse reminds you of this goodness and makes you want to dance and laugh with deep relief that we are, in fact, the object of God's affection.

- What is noisy in your life right now? What are the messages you're taking in about who you are or how you measure up?

- What would it look like to take some of that noise away and tune into the song God sings over you?

- Try to imagine the chorus of the song God might be singing over you and write it down here. Ask Him to show you how He delights in you and listen to what He might bring to your mind and heart.

Oh God, what a gift it is to know that You delight in each of your children, including me. You are the singer of songs over not just Your family as a whole, but me specifically! Would You help me to tune into the songs You sing? Thank You for singing over me from the mountaintops to the valleys. Thank You for the ways you quiet me with Your love. Would You help me to turn up the volume of the song of love You're singing over me, and dance for the joy of knowing I am Your beloved child? Help me to turn the volume up on the song of love You sing over others as well, and give me the strength to join in the chorus.

"For I am the LORD your God who takes
hold of your right hand and says to you,
Do not fear; I will help you."

ISAIAH 41:13

Do you ever feel like you are carrying ALL THE THINGS? Gripping tight, exhausted, and trying to hold it all together for both yourself and the people around you? Me too. I am not great at asking for help, and I often end up running myself into the ground because I just keep trying to muster up the strength/faith/courage to keep going. This is exhausting, and I'm reminded by this verse that I don't have to carry on like that. What a relief to know that even when we are dropping all the balls, losing our minds, feeling weak, full of doubt or fear, plagued with anxiety or loneliness, God has a firm grip on us. He isn't letting go. We don't have to panic, because we have a kind and capable Helper. I love how Eugene Peterson puts this verse: "That's right. Because I, your God, have a firm grip on you and I'm not letting go. I'm telling you, 'Don't panic. I'm right here to help you'" (MSG).

I ran across this beautiful verse when I was writing "I Will Carry You" with Ben Glover. We had set out to write a song for our children. I want all of my kids to know in the depths of their being that they are not alone, and that I'll be forever in their corner, so "I Will Carry You" was born. At first the whole focus was making sure *my kids* knew this truth, but when I ran across this promise in God's Word, all of the sudden it shifted this song for me . . . It reminded me once again that before I'm a mother or adult trying to carry all the things—including my children—I'm God's kid, and He is an ever-present source of love and help and hope that will carry *me* when it feels like I can't carry on any longer. And even though He's given me the job of raising up my children, He has a firm grip on them too.

I'm deeply grateful for this beautiful truth, and I hope this verse will forever be a reminder to you that you will NEVER walk alone, and that you can fall apart in the arms of the One who holds all things together. Love will carry those you love through, yes. But don't forget—Love will carry you through too. I hope the lyrics to "I Will Carry You" remind you of the beautiful truth of God's constant, steadfast love.

> *I will carry you through your darkest night*
> *When you're terrified*
> *I will carry you, when the waters rise*
> *When your hope runs dry*
> *I will carry you*[8]

What I didn't know when I wrote the song grounded in this Scripture is that on the very day we'd be making the music video for "I Will Carry You," I'd find out that our pastor and his child were tragically killed in a car accident. It's the kind of news that shatters you and sends you reeling, sobbing, asking God, "WHY?!?" I was deeply grieving that day. I'm still grieving the loss of those two beautiful souls, but as I sang this song over and over again, it reminded me there is a God whose love is strong enough to carry us through deep seasons of grief. There is a God who carries us from the grave, into life everlasting. There is a God who weeps with us as we break, and who holds us together when we are falling apart. *Oh God, thank You for the way that we never have to panic or carry any burden or grief alone. You are faithful to carry us now and forever.*

- What are you carrying in this season?

- How does it make you feel to know that God will carry you no matter what you might be carrying?

- What might you be able to let go of and trust into His care, knowing that He is a faithful helper?

I carry so much in my heart and in my life, Lord. Thank you that I don't ever carry any of it alone. Thank you that when I can't carry on, I can trust that You've got a firm grip on me and that You'll never let me go. When my heart starts to race or I begin to feel waves of anxiety, weariness, worry, or grief settle in, would You help me to take a deep breath and remember that You are holding me, even there? Thank You that You are an ever-present help to me. Help me to keep leaning on Your everlasting arms as I trust you to carry me and everything else in my life and my heart.

Praise the LORD, my soul; all my inmost being,
praise his holy name.
Praise the LORD, my soul, and forget not all his benefits—
who forgives all your sins and heals all your diseases,
who redeems your life from the pit and
crowns you with love and compassion,
who satisfies your desires with good things so
that your youth is renewed like the eagle's.

PSALM 103:1–5

This is one of the first verses I ever memorized because it's one of the first verses I ever set to a melody. It has brought my soul deep comfort over and over again, so when I read through the original *Fighting Words* after it was printed and realized I hadn't included it, I just knew I had to add it to this special edition.

I was fresh out of college when I first read these beautiful words from Psalm 103, and I remember it stirring up a deep longing for the gift of remembering. I wanted to help my forgetful soul remember God's love for me, and this verse has been like a balm to apply to my soul, especially during seasons of doubt and loss. "Forget not all His benefits!" I LOVE this phrase.

I've sung this Scripture in the wake of making terrible decisions and struggling to move forward under the weight of the shame of them.

Forget not: "He forgives all of your sins."

I've sung this Scripture while longing for healing for family members who were sick, trying to remind myself that healing will come whether it's on this side of glory or the next.

Forget not: "He heals all your diseases."

I've sung this Scripture in the darkest nights of my soul, when it felt like the pit of sorrow and anxiety was too deep to ever get out.

Forget not: "He redeems your life from the pit."

I've sung this Scripture when I have had major battles with self-image and insecurity. It has reminded me that no matter what I look like or how I compare to anyone else, that I am beloved of God.

Forget not: "He crowns you with love."

I've sung this Scripture over each of my kids while they were growing in my belly, praying that God will help them know His love in the deepest places in their hearts.

Forget not: "Praise the Lord, oh my soul, and all my inmost being."

I've sung it over my heart that was longing for answers to prayers and desires, feeling unseen and unlistened-to by God, and not understanding why things weren't turning out the way I hoped.

Forget not: "He satisfies your desires with good things."

(God satisfying me with good things hasn't always looked like I thought it would, but I cannot think of a single scenario when God's love hasn't been enough to sustain me.)

And I'm weeping now as I remember all the days it felt like doubt would drown me. This passage has been like a life raft, keeping me afloat, filling me with the hope of God's love that shines brighter than any darkness or doubt we'll ever face. It has anchored me when it felt like winds of shame and sorrow would surely sink the ship. And it has lifted me up on eagle's wings to heights I never dreamed of or imagined. It has been a Scripture that has renewed my soul over and over again.

Oh God, our work is to remember. Help us to FORGET NOT all Your benefits and THANK YOU for the way You have used this verse over and over again in my life to whisper to my doubting heart about Your kindness and love for me. Come, even now, and whisper again.

- What do you want to FORGET NOT? Take a moment to write down ways God has loved you and met you in all kinds of seasons.

- What is one benefit of the love of God that you want to hold onto today?

What particular characteristic of God do you most often forget? How does remembering His character shift where your heart is?

Help me to remember well, God, especially on the days when doubt and shame come rolling in like a storm front, shaking me to my core. May I "forget not" all Your benefits and remember that I get to walk the earth with a crown of Your love on my head. May this remembering of Your love shape every decision I make, every word I say, and everything that I do. May I move through this broken world as a person who remembers and drinks deeply of Your love, and who pours out that same love wherever I go.

If you'd like to sing this psalm with me, it's written into the song called "Don't Forget His Love" on my album, *All of My Days*.

Your word is a lamp for my feet, a light on my path.

PSALM 119:105

This little verse from Psalm 119 is printed on the back of this book. It's yet another verse I couldn't believe I hadn't included in the original 100 days of *Fighting Words*. I was eight years old when I had the privilege of walking into an arena full of people singing this verse at the top of their lungs. It was an Amy Grant concert, my first, and I was undone by that moment. Maybe you remember the encouragement it offers—that when we're deeply afraid that we've somehow lost our way, God is there right beside us. That we don't have to be thrown by fear as long as God is near—which He is!—and we can trust that He's with us to the very end. And I'll never forget that memorable refrain wrapped in that beautiful melody straight from the Word of God: "Thy word is a lamp unto my feet and a light unto my path" (KJV).

When I heard this powerful song, something beautiful was stirred up in my eight-year-old heart that night. I was witnessing a room full of people who were singing with all of their souls about the comfort and light that God's Word could bring. It brings me to tears because I've had the gift of that comfort and light for all the years of my life. In so many ways, that is what these pages hold: the words of God that have brought light and hope to some of the darkest places along my journey.

Fast-forward from eight-year-old me being massively impacted at an Amy Grant concert, to college: I went on a hike in the Smoky Mountains with a friend to watch the sun set over the hills. It seemed like a great idea. We could enjoy the sun setting and then catch the first few glimmers of stars before hiking back down. It was a great night. We enjoyed conversation as we took in all the beauty around us. When it was time to head back down, I stood up and suddenly had a pit in my stomach. The realization hit me that I had completely forgotten to pack a *flashlight* in my backpack. Thankfully, my friend had a head lamp, but it was *dark* and we had to hike over three miles back to the car.

I'll never forget it . . . following each foot step, one move, one step at a time, straining my eyes to see the next dimly-lit portion of our path. We moved slowly for about twenty minutes and then something terrible happened. The headlamp started to flicker on and off as we walked. As I was trying not to LOSE IT, my friend pulled the batteries out and put them back in again. We didn't have any extras. We kept moving, slowly, with a light as dim as a match that kept going in and out with every step we took. Finally, as we clambered over a big tree that had fallen across the trail, the headlamp went out completely. We were plunged into darkness. We stopped walking.

At this point, I wish I could say that I was brave and kept myself cool and collected, but this would not be true. My heart was POUNDING. I couldn't see my hand in front of my face, and the worst part? Once we stopped hiking, we could not only hear animals moving through the woods all around us—we could see *glowing eyes* of some of those animals! I wanted to scream. Tears were streaming down my face. I did NOT sing "Thy Word" in this moment. I did NOT hold onto a Scripture to help calm my pounding heart. But I did pray. I begged God to help us.

My friend was rifling through the backpack we brought, which happened to have a box of matches. Sometimes, God really does answer prayer. We tried striking the match to get our bearings. For a brief moment, we could see the trail stretching out before us, narrow and covered with fallen trees and roots, but then the light snuffed out and we could see nothing as we smelled the smoking wood of the match. We decided to light another and try to gather anything we could use to pull together a make-shift torch.

We fashioned a stick with grass wrapped around the end and lit it, hoping it would light up with a bright flame to show everything around us. But when we lit it, it burned instead like a low-glowing ember, giving us just enough light to take each step. On the last mile, thanks be to God, the clouds cleared and the moon came out, acting like a flashlight from heaven! We picked up our pace to a run and *finally* made it back to the car. I burst into tears when we did.

I'll never forget that night—the way I needed the light desperately to move forward and make my way back home. This is how I've felt about God's promises. They have been like a comforting, glowing ember as I move forward—a sweet relief when I've felt lost in the dark. And they shine brighter than the darkness that has engulfed me from time to time. They have led me, step by step, like a light on my path and a lamp to my feet back home to the truth of God's love and provision for me. God's promises have helped scatter the darkest lies I've been tempted to believe with the light of the truth of God's love for me.

As we leave our time together in this special edition of *Fighting Words*, I pray that every Scripture passage in this book would be the same for you, like ever accessible lamps that will shine brighter than a makeshift torch when you lose your way. I pray that they would give you the hope and wisdom and comfort you're desperate for, and that they would light up the path back into the arms of the One who made you and knows you best.

— The moment I realized the value and gift of God's Word was at that Amy Grant concert. Do you have a moment in your life where you fell in love with Scripture, or realized its worth?

— Have you ever walked through a season marked by darkness, emotionally or spiritually? Or are you perhaps walking on a path that feels confusing or dark right now? If so, what "makeshift torch" do you usually turn to, to help you make it through?

— Can you think of some Scripture that has been like a lamp for your feet? If so, write it out right now and recount the stories of how it has guided you back to Love. If not, ask the Lord to bring a Scripture to mind that you could memorize and use like a lamp to guide you home. Write it here and start trying to bury that light in your heart!

Oh God, thank You for your Word. Thank You for the Living Word, Jesus, who is the Light of the World, who never leaves me, even through the darkest nights of my soul. May I be quick to hold onto Your promises, especially when I am drowning in darkness and in the lies that lead me to believe I'm all alone. Let Your Word guide me back into Your loving arms, and let it transform even the darkest places of my story into moments washed in Your light. May my heart be made more like Yours as I keep holding on to Your Word and as I keep remembering You are always holding onto me. Thank You that light is always stronger than the darkness. Help me continue to bury Your Word, Your light, Your love, deep in my heart, so that I am anchored and grounded and covered by Your love and Your promises. And as I ground myself in Your Word, may I shine Your light and love into this dark and weary world, and move through the earth as an agent of hope and healing. Lead me on, with Your light and love, oh God, and replace every lie I've ever believed with the truth of Your love for me.

If you'd like to sing this psalm with me, it's featured in a cover I did of "Thy Word" by Amy Grant on my album, *All of My Days*.

NOTES

1. C. S. Lewis, *The Lion, the Witch, and the Wardrobe* (New York: HarperCollins, 1950), 86, emphasis added.

2. See J. R. R. Tolkien, *The Return of the King,* Book 3 of The Lord of the Rings series (New York: Houghton Mifflin Harcourt, 1955).

3. Timothy Keller, *Making Sense of God* Reading Plan, Day 3, https://www.bible.com/es/reading-plans/3095-making-sense-of-god-timothy-keller/day/3.

4. *Thayer's Greek Lexicon*, Electronic Database. Copyright © 2002, 2003, 2006, 2011 by Biblesoft, Inc. All rights reserved. Used by permission. BibleSoft.com, "STRONGS NT 4151: πνεῦμα," https://biblehub.com/greek/4151.htm.

5. Richard Rohr, "First Sunday of Advent: Come, Lord Jesus," December 1, 2019, https://www.franciscanmedia.org/franciscan-spirit-blog/first-sunday-of-advent-come-lord-jesus.

6. https://www.lexico.com/definition/consolation

7. Michael Card, *John: The Gospel of Wisdom* (Downers Grove, IL: InterVarsity Press, 2014), 36.

8. "I Will Carry You," lyrics by Ellie Holcomb. (Full Heart Music/Capitol CMG Genesis) and Ben Glover (9t One Songs/Ariose Music), used with permission.

ALSO AVAILABLE FROM
ELLIE HOLCOMB

AVAILABLE WHERE BOOKS ARE SOLD